Latin American Economic History

Latin American Economic History: An Introduction to Daily Life, Debt, and Development guides readers through significant features and developments in the region's economic history from independence through 2022.

In approachable language, the book introduces readers to relevant New Economic History concepts and explains important characteristics of Latin America, such as the region's high volatility, rapid urbanization experience, the continued prominence of commodities, and its culture of informality. The volume provides explicit connections between culture, politics, and economics over five distinct time periods. Readers will learn how Cinco de Mayo featured in foreign debt repayments in the nineteenth century, how novels like Gabriel García Márquez's *One Hundred Years of Solitude* reflected on the expansion of railroads during a period of export-led growth, and how a United States federal reserve interest hike in 1979 sent the region into the Lost Decade. When considered collectively, the region's economic trajectory demonstrates that development does not always accompany economic growth.

This is an accessible introductory text with clear definitions and discussions of relevant economic concepts, which will be a valuable resource for students of Latin American economic, cultural, and political history.

Molly C. Ball teaches history and coordinates Latin American Studies at the University of Rochester. Her monograph, *Navigating Life and Work in Old Republic São Paulo* (2020), and scholarship examine the intersections of economic and social history by exploring how large macro events impacted people's daily lives and experiences.

Latin American Tópicos

Latin American Tópicos
Edited by Michael LaRosa, Rhodes College

Telenovelas in Pan-Latino Context
June Carolyn Erlick

The Youngest Citizens
Amy Risley

Latin American Soldiers
Armed Forces in the Region's History
John R. Bawden

Natural Disasters in Latin America and the Caribbean
Coping with Calamity
June Carolyn Erlick

Public Health and Beyond in Latin America and the Caribbean
Reflections from the Field
Sherri L. Porcelain

Essays on 20th Century Latin American Art
Francine Birbragher-Rozencwaig

Latin American Economic History
An Introduction to Daily Life, Debt, and Development
Molly C. Ball

For more information about this series, please visit:
www.routledge.com/Latin-American-Tpicos/book-series/LAT

Latin American Economic History

An Introduction to Daily Life, Debt, and Development

Molly C. Ball

Designed cover image: Left: Manual harvesting of sugar cane in rural Orlandia. Pulsar Imagens/Alamy Stock Photo. Right: Cusco Train – Peru Rails in Black and White. Gary Vargas/Alamy Stock Photo

First published 2025
by Routledge
605 Third Avenue, New York, NY 10158

and by Routledge
4 Park Square, Milton Park, Abingdon, Oxon, OX14 4RN

Routledge is an imprint of the Taylor & Francis Group, an informa business

ISBN: 978-1-032-25546-0 (hbk)
ISBN: 978-1-032-22434-3 (pbk)
ISBN: 978-1-003-28384-3 (ebk)

DOI: 10.4324/9781003283843

Typeset in Sabon
by Deanta Global Publishing Services, Chennai, India

To Dr. Steven Marks, my forever model of what a professor and mentor should be, and to Pablo, whose unwavering support and faith make projects like this possible.

Contents

Acknowledgments

Each semester I have the privilege of bringing economic history to life for the students enrolled in my courses. *Latin American Economic History* now provides me with an incredible opportunity to share those insights and my enthusiasm with a broader audience. Doing so, however, would have been impossible without the patient support of the Tópicos editors, the enthusiasm and feedback from colleagues, the cadre of mentors who have fostered my love of Latin American economic history, and the support of family and friends.

I thank John Bawden for introducing me to Routledge's Tópicos series and the managing editor, Michael LaRosa. Mike has provided guidance and valuable feedback from the first stages of this project in Spring 2021 through the final manuscript submission three years later. Neither of us could have foreseen the incredible challenges that COVID-19 would bring to the process, but he has been patient and supportive, as have Taylor & Francis managing editors, Allison Sambucini and Kimberley Smith. Emily Irvine also provided key assistance at Taylor & Francis. I am equally indebted to the University of Rochester for their support. A grant to support faculty impacted by COVID-19 facilitated summer writing, and I thank the library and the General Research Fund of the University of Rochester's history department for generously providing the funding to make *Latin American Economic History* open access. Lara Nicosia ensured that the request made its way to Lindsay Cronk, who was a key advocate for making this project available to a wide audience. Sharon Briggs continued that support, as did Ruben Flores in the history department.

Sandra Mendiola García and José Juan Pérez Meléndez provided valuable feedback on the project in its initial stages. They challenged me to consider alternate timeframes and championed the book's contribution to the existing scholarship. As I worked through the challenges of covering such an enormous topic in an approachable and succinct way, I looked to their comments for motivation. During the writing stage, several chapters benefited from comments and suggestions from workshops with the

University of Rochester's history department and the Humanities Center's GRUPO working group. Feedback from Jeffrey Baron, Claire Becker, Vialcary Crisóstomo, Ruben Flores, John Kapusta, Rachel O'Donnell, Ryan Prendergast, Luisa Maria Rojas-Rimachi, Matt Lenoe, Pablo Sierra Silva, and Alice Wynd proved particularly helpful. I must also thank my students, who listened to versions of this book in lecture form. Their reactions were critical in demonstrating terms and concepts that needed further clarification, and I thank Daniel Guerra for providing solicited feedback from a student perspective. Blair Tinker proved instrumental in helping to create figures and Rio Hartwell's bibliographic assistance was critical. Sebastián Cordero Velastegui assisted with research early on, tracking down missing literacy rates and scouring newspaper databases to find connections to personalize the numbers and major trends that can make economic history seem faceless.

This book benefited from a range of intellectual discussions and debates. An invitation from Silvana Maubrigades and María Camou to participate in a *Revista Uruguaya de História Económica* special issue dedicated to analyzing how crises impact women helped me identify breaking points and define development. Sections related to (im)migration and labor benefited considerably from co-planning and participating in the Mellon Foundation's Sawyer seminar series hosted at the University of Rochester from 2020 to 2022, "Unbordering Migration in the Americas: Causes, Experiences, Identities." I thank my co-organizers and the distinguished scholars and community members who participated in the series for sharing their time and knowledge. More recently, discussions from the Johns Hopkins University "Genealogies of Development" workshop were instrumental in revising several chapters. Casey Lurtz's leadership and collegiality in organizing that workshop deserve special thanks.

The intellectual trajectory of this project, however, began much earlier. Twenty years ago, Dr. Steven Marks introduced me to economic history in a "History of Capitalism" seminar at Clemson University. I have been hooked ever since and he has continued along the ride as a mentor. As a graduate student at UCLA, I benefited from dynamic dialogues that brought historians and economists into weekly conversations. Bill Summerhill, Naomi Lamoreaux, the late Ken Sokoloff, and Leah Boustan became key mentors, and ensured that I benefited from the camaraderie of the UCLA economic history proseminar, the VonGremp workshop, and the all-UC economic history group. These groups nurtured my commitment to understand the historical intersections between economics and everyday life. Anne Hanley and Joel Wolfe have also served as supportive mentors through the years. Luís Bértola proved incredibly supportive at a critical point, when I was presenting to a hostile audience as a young graduate student. While researching in Brazil, Elizabeth Johnson, Renato

Colistete, and his economic history working group have always provided this much-needed intellectual dialogue. When I first arrived at Rochester, the late Stan Engerman was a champion of economic history and my colleagues in the history department have always been welcoming.

Finally, I would like to thank my family. Brennen, Cuauhtemoc, and Carolina – your conversations and questions always keep me on my toes and are often very insightful. You provide hugs and distractions at just the right time. Pablo, you are always my greatest cheerleader and have always found value in what I do. As a colleague, you share my enthusiasm to bring our work to a broader audience, but as a spouse, you deftly navigate our work-life balance so that we meet not just our academic but also our life goals. I hope that one day, when our kids read *Latin American Economic History* and *Mexico, Slavery, Freedom*, they will fondly recall the teamwork that goes into making knowledge happen.

1 Growth vs. Development

Twenty minutes into Luis Buñuel's classic Mexican film *Los Olvidados* (1950), translated as *The Young and the Damned*, a meeting between three adolescent boys leaves one dead, another on a tragic path toward a lifetime of injustice, and a third unchanged, stealing from and exploiting those around him. As El Jaibo threatens Julian and Pedro watches on, the framing of a high-rise building with steel beams stands prominently in the background. It is next to other modern buildings, which provide a stark contrast throughout the film to the shanty and informal structures where the boys live.

Buñuel's film was renowned for its surrealism and psychological storyline, and he even won best director at the Cannes film festival.[1] The film's raw portrayal of Latin American poverty made it emblematic of a period of cinematic history that would adhere to similar principles. Connecting stories like those portrayed in *Los Olivdados* to broader trends in Latin American economic history is the aim of this book. Buñuel's ability to make such a polemic film was intricately connected to the region's economic trajectory. In an effort to compete with Hollywood and other foreign film industries, Latin America's largest countries began actively developing their own film industries in the 1930s. It was with substantial governmental support that Mexico entered its golden age of cinema. Such state intervention also helps to explain the high-rise building in the background of this pivotal scene, as state-led growth did not start or stop with the film industry. The 1940s in Mexico and throughout the region saw national efforts to diversify production and increase industrial capacity in an attempt to catch up to more developed nations. The period also saw increased migrations to urban centers as mechanization and land accumulation restricted agricultural workers.

Given the tragic developments that continue throughout the film, viewers may be tempted to wonder if the mid-twentieth century represented a low point in Mexico City. A secondary character in the film offers some insight into this question. A blind, old accordion peddler laments the state

DOI: 10.4324/9781003283843-1

of life, nostalgically yearning for the years of nineteenth-century dictator Porfirio Díaz. But was the earlier era any better? In the Díaz years, a period where exports dominated the national vision, Mexico, like the rest of the region, did see substantial growth. So theoretically, in his youth, he might have experienced some great benefits. However, his subsequent suffering offers a cautionary reading: Latin American growth left many people behind.

Country Groups

Latin America as a region includes 20 countries, each with unique economic and social circumstances. Spanish is the most commonly spoken language; but in Brazil, Portuguese is the lingua franca; in Haiti, Krèyol dominates; and in many countries, Indigenous languages survive and even thrive in certain regions. The climate also varies dramatically, including temperate plateau regions, tropical rainforests, pine forests, grasslands, deserts, and every variation in between. Cultural histories are equally diverse, providing rich traditions that often combine European, African, and Indigenous practices and beliefs. Despite the region's diversity, synthesizing these national histories into subgroups allows for a cohesive approach to the region's economic history.

Scholars often organize the region into two groups. Argentina, Brazil, Chile, Colombia, Mexico, and Uruguay constitute one group, and the remaining 14 medium and small-size countries constitute a second group. Bértola and Ocampo propose that appropriate country groupings vary across time and require more nuanced subdivisions.[2] For the period from independence in the early nineteenth century through 1930, they describe four subgroups based on the country's nineteenth-century export structure and the dominant labor force during the period – Indigenous-descended, African-descended, or European-descended populations (see Table 1.1). For the post-1930 period, the size of the national economy takes on additional significance in defining subgroups of small, medium, and large countries (see Figure 1.1).

The nineteenth-century labor categorizations are impossible to understand without a brief overview of colonial Latin American labor exploitation and land structure.[3] Prior to European colonization, Indigenous communities inhabited the region. Semi-sedentary populations geographically were the most prominent, but in the Andean highlands, central Mexico, and the Yucatan peninsula, sedentary, hierarchical populations flourished. For example, in 1519, when Hernán Cortés arrived in Tenochtitlán, the seat of the Aztec Empire, its population exceeded that of London. In other words, there were key colonial **factor endowment** distinctions, or differences between the *existing natural resources, soil, labor, and capital capabilities* within Latin America even prior to the colonial period, particularly in terms of labor. The Conquest decimated many of these populations, and by the end of the sixteenth century the population in the Americas had fallen from around 50 million to just over 5 million people. Conquistadors, missionaries, servants, and enslaved people brought deadly diseases like smallpox and influenza, proving to be colonization's deadliest consequence for America's Indigenous populations. Massive depopulation did not end labor exploitation. Rather there was increased dependence on African slavery by way of the transatlantic slave trade that continued in some countries into the post-independence era. Between 1500 and 1866, over 9 million enslaved Africans disembarked in Latin America.[4] In colonial times, Black and Indigenous populations, and their descendants, tended to vastly outnumber Europeans, a tendency that continued into the national period.

In spaces where there had been large, sedentary Indigenous populations prior to the Conquest and in surrounding regions, *mestizo*, mixed populations implying a degree of Indigenous origin, and Indigenous workers came to perform the bulk of labor in the national period. This was the case for Mexico, Guatemala, El Salvador, Honduras, Nicaragua, Colombia, Venezuela, Bolivia, Ecuador, Peru, Chile, and Paraguay. The presence of nineteenth-century mining exports further subdivided this group. During the colonial era, Latin American silver and gold financed Iberian wars, imperialism, and Renaissance construction. As new independent nations, and amidst growing global industrialization that required mined materials, mining was also crucial to the Mexican, Colombian, Bolivian, Peruvian, and Chilean economies in the nineteenth century. These countries shared a similar economic trajectory between independence and 1930 due to exports like silver, gold, tin, and copper. For the countries without a central mining export – Paraguay, Ecuador, Nicaragua, El Salvador, Honduras, and Guatemala – agricultural exports and peasant agriculture defined the nineteenth-century labor experience.

In areas of Latin America that lacked a large, sedentary Indigenous colonial population, or where European diseases effectively eliminated the population, as was the case with the Caribbean, Africans and Afro-descended populations came to provide the bulk of labor in the colonial and post-colonial period. Many of these individuals were enslaved, working to cultivate tropical agricultural products for export, like sugar and cacao. Tropical products were more profitable if cultivated on large, landed estates. This profit seeking increased chattel slavery and further concentrated land and export wealth in the hands of elites. This was the reality not only for inhabitants in the Caribbean (the independent nations of the Dominican Republic and Haiti, and the Spanish colonies of Cuba and Puerto Rico), but also in Brazil, Venezuela, and Panama.[5] These countries, along with Costa Rica, constitute the third group.[6]

The region's southernmost countries, known as the Southern Cone (Argentina, Uruguay, Chile, and parts of Brazil), constitute the fourth and final subgroup for the period from independence through 1930. During the colonial period, these areas were largely peripheral zones. More difficult to reach by transportation, labor was also scarcer. Exploitation and Indigenous and chattel slavery did exist in these spaces, but peripheral conditions provided more opportunities for social mobility. Temperate-zone agriculture also flourished here, incentivizing the subregion to adopt more equitable land distribution. By the middle of the nineteenth century, a sizeable number of new European colonists and immigrants arrived, becoming the dominant nineteenth-century labor force.

As Table 1.1 demonstrates, some overlap exists between the groups. In Venezuela and Colombia, for example, African-descended populations and tropical agriculture dominated coastal areas, while highland areas concentrated Indigenous-descended groups and a mining sector. Chile, on the other hand, had a strong mining sector and deep Indigenous roots, but it also shared a similar trajectory to other Southern Cone nations in the latter half of the nineteenth century. Brazil's southern and portions of its southeast regions are also more closely related to the Southern Cone experience in the late nineteenth and early twentieth centuries. Therefore, parts of Brazil also fit within two groups.

As global trade expanded and production rose and diversified, the size of a country's economy took on added significance. From 1930 forward, considering countries in terms of small, medium, and large economies is helpful in making economic trajectory generalizations. This classification holds true for economic indicators related to industrial growth, diversification, and **gross domestic product per capita,** *the amount of goods and services*

Table 1.1 Latin American subgroups: Independence–1930

Dominant nineteenth-century labor and export product structure	*Countries*
Indigenous and *mestizo* labor force and mining exports	Mexico, Colombia, Bolivia, Peru, Chile, Venezuela
Indigenous and *mestizo* labor and subsistence agriculture or agricultural exports	Paraguay, Ecuador, Nicaragua, El Salvador, Honduras, Guatemala
Afro-descended labor and tropical agricultural exports	Brazil, Venezuela, Panama, Colombia, Dominican Republic, Haiti, Cuba,* Puerto Rico,* Costa Rica**
European-descended labor and temperate agriculture	Argentina, Uruguay, Chile, Brazil

Notes: * For most of the 19th century, Cuba and Puerto Rico remained Spanish colonies.
**Costa Rica predominantly relied on European-descended labor.

produced by a country divided by its population. Other quality-of-life indicators, like infant mortality and literacy, seem to follow the first typology related to colonial labor structures and natural endowments. Most countries in the region are classified as small economies. Peru, Colombia, and Venezuela are medium-sized economies, while Brazil, the ninth largest global economy, and Mexico constitute large economies. The one exception is the Southern Cone region, where Chile (medium), Argentina (medium), and Uruguay (small) continue to share similar features.

Economic Growth vs. Economic Development

Economic history is often concerned with growth and development, two terms that are intimately intertwined, but not synonymous. Growth occurs when the amount of goods or services that a country produces increases. The meaning of development has changed over time. As a constructed term, changing societal values and goals mean that what development meant in the nineteenth century is not necessarily consistent with our current understanding of development. This book will use the United Nations' **human development index** (HDI) as the entry point for discussing development. Since the 1990s, scholars have used the metric as the leading *indicator of development.* HDI *averages life expectancy, years of schooling, and income per capita for each country, allowing for comparisons across nations and regions.*[7] The augmented human development index goes one step further to acknowledge that the HDI index cannot fully represent choices and persistent inequities, noting moments of restricted political freedoms and persistent inequities.[8]

Economic growth is usually required for economic development, but economic growth can occur without or with minimal development. Since independence, Latin America has enjoyed economic growth; however, gains to development have often been lackluster. On the individual level this means that the typical inhabitant in Latin America enjoyed a better quality of life than the generation before them, but that those improvements should have been even higher. Regional failures to redistribute wealth and resources mean that Latin American countries fared poorly compared to other countries with similar incomes in terms of indicators like infant mortality rates, educational achievements, and labor force participation.

Population growth is one of the main drivers of economic growth, but cultivating a new crop, opening a new factory, a new technology, and expanding the service industry can also result in GDP growth. When the total value of production grows faster than the population, a country's gross domestic product per capita (GDP/capita) increases. Theoretically, these new revenues could distribute these gains across the population. For example, if farmers successfully plant, grow, and sell an additional crop, this brings in a new source of income for the farmers. Workers on the farm

Figure 1.1 Map of modern Latin America by economy size, 1930–2022. The economy size of Puerto Rico and Belize are not included as the former is a territory of the United States and the latter is a former British colony.

also have the potential to gain, depending on whether the farm owners raise wages or offer bonuses or services to the labor force. The government can also make gains by either levying a tax on exports, a sales tax, or a tax on the agriculturalists' profits. The government can then use the money from these taxes to provide goods and services to the population at large, such as building or improving schools, roads, or infrastructure. The new crop has made a bigger pie, but it has also increased the size of the pie for everyone.

In Latin America, the pie has continued to get bigger, but some slices have grown while others have shrunk. Between 1820 and 2008, the region's economy grew steadily, albeit at a slower pace than economies in Western Europe, Australia, the United States, and Canada (the West). Latin America's share of global GDP also increased considerably, from just 1.9 percent in 1820 to 7.8 percent in 2008. Population growth explains much of Latin America's GDP growth, but GDP per capita also increased tenfold.[9] Figure 1.2 shows how Latin America fared relative to the West and the rest of the world. At independence the region's GDP per capita was just over half of that for Western countries. Since independence Latin American performance relative to the West has steadily declined.

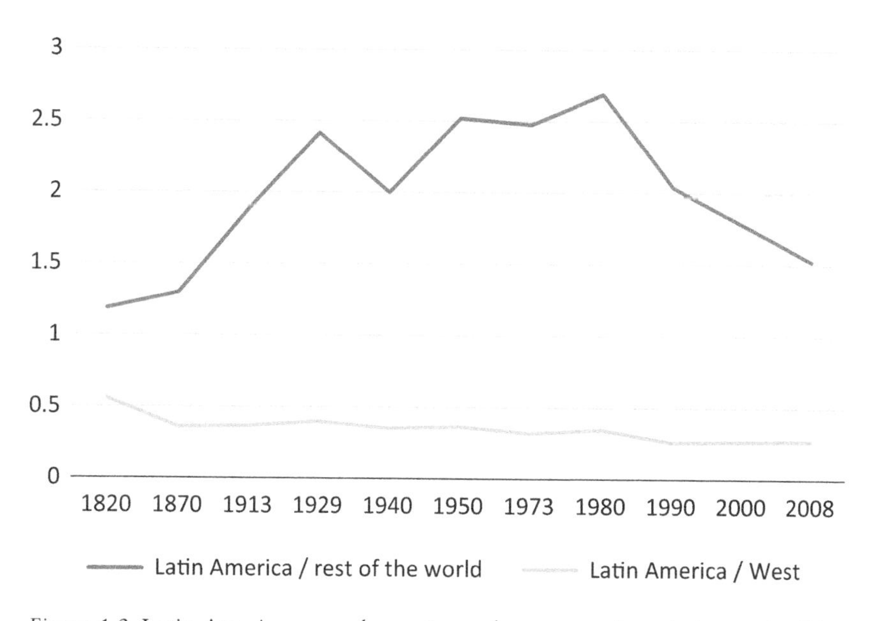

Figure 1.2 Latin America gross domestic product per capita relative to the West and the world, 1820–2008. Graph elaborated from Bértola and Ocampo, *Economic Development of Latin America*, table 1.1, pp. 4–5.

Notes: The West is the equivalent of 12 Western European countries, Australia, Canada, United States, and New Zealand. Latin America does not include Haiti.

Its performance relative to the rest of the world has been more varied. Relative GDP per capita largely improved from independence to 1930 and after World War II through 1980. The interwar years, however, represented a relative decline as did the 1980s. Since that period the region has continued to outperform African economies, but East Asian economies have outpaced Latin American growth, and by 2008, many of Latin America's gains from the earlier periods had eroded.

What goods and services contributed to the GDP growth in Figure 1.2? This is an important question to answer because exploring what is produced rather than how much is an alternative way to consider growth and, arguably, development. Diversifying production to include a wide range of goods and services helps reduce economic volatility, a problem that plagues modern Latin American economic history. This is because if a country relies too heavily on producing one or just a few types of goods, its economy is susceptible to any market changes associated with those goods. This high volatility impacts everything from prices to migration, making it difficult for governments to fund national budgets and complicating entrepreneurs' and consumers' planning for the future.

There are two additional challenges Latin America has faced relative to export good prices. The first is the **terms of trade** volatility experienced when the *price countries received for exports relative to the prices they paid for imports* fluctuated. Say a country exports wheat and imports screws. When wheat prices are high relative to screws, then the country can import more screws. However, if wheat prices drop, even if screw prices do not shift, the wheat-producing country will have to reduce the number of screws imported. Since the late nineteenth century, terms of trade price variations in Latin America have become more dramatic and shifted more quickly, adding to the region's economic volatility.

A key reason for this volatility is that certain products are more susceptible to price fluctuations than others. Goods fall into categories based on their function and who uses them. **Primary goods** *are sold for consumption and are grown or found naturally*. From wheat and bananas to mined materials like copper and tin, these are also known as **commodities**.[10] There are **intermediate goods,** *the materials or ingredients needed to make finished products*. Some commodities, like metals and agricultural products, can also be intermediate goods, while others, like nails, screws, and cloth, are processed primary goods. **Capital goods** are *the buildings, machines, and tools needed to create a product*. Finally, **consumer goods** are *things that people buy and use directly, like clothes, appliances, food, televisions, and books*. If we use a chocolate chip cookie analogy, intermediate goods, like sugar and chocolate chips, are the ingredients (in this case, sugar is also a commodity), the capital goods are the mixer and oven, and the consumer good is the final cookie.

To produce any of these goods requires four different elements: land, labor, capital, and entrepreneurship. Very few countries have the physical size (land), natural resources (raw materials), or manpower (labor) to specialize in every area. Every country has limited resources (capital) to allocate to production. So, deciding whether to produce T-shirts or oranges can be a complex calculation that entails weighing economic possibilities alongside political and social considerations. Much of colonial-era Latin America was rich in the factor endowments of land. Mining and tropical agricultural economies flourished, albeit often on the backs of enslaved African and exploited Indigenous laborers. In the nineteenth century, as Latin American nations became independent, agricultural and raw material production expanded in the region. With fertile soils and low population density, Latin America was a land-rich region, poised to produce and export commodities to an expanding global market in exchange for consumer and capital goods and services.

This export market, or the selling of products and services to other nations, complemented the existing **domestic market,** *the goods and services produced within and for the national population.* Given their natural resources, Latin American economies have often specialized in producing and exporting agricultural products and raw materials. Unfortunately, these products are often the most susceptible to market shocks. A drought, a bumper crop, a war, or the entry of another producer and competitor has almost immediate and large price effects. This volatility means sometimes countries experience periods of remarkable GDP growth. For example, increased demand for metals like tin and copper during World War II (1938–1945) led to extraordinary growth in Bolivia and Chile. These periods, however, are often followed by prices bottoming out or currency, banking, and debt crises. In Latin America, such economic instability often exacerbates structural social inequities and has frequently contributed to burgeoning political crises. Brazilian rubber at the turn of the twentieth century provides a good case study. In 1910, Brazil produced the majority of the world's rubber, but when British plantations in Malaysia successfully began producing rubber from smuggled *Havea Brasiliensis* seeds, Brazil's global market share dropped to just 11 percent. Almost overnight, infrastructure growth in Brazil's Amazon region slowed considerably.

Finding a new resource is also sometimes associated with "**Dutch disease.**" Contrary to what is expected by its name, the term can be applied across regions and time periods. It refers to a *phenomenon where countries or colonies invest resources in the infrastructure and production in a new sector, often a newly found natural resource. At the same point, the exchange rate appreciates due to the interest in the new sector, disincentivizing investment in other sectors, often manufacturing or agriculture within the country.* With a higher exchange rate, imported products are cheaper. When prices for the new sector or industry drop, the fallout is considerable. Growing new natural resource production does not necessarily result in Dutch disease, but Chile's development of nitrates in the late nineteenth and Venezuela's oil sector in the twenty-first centuries offer just two examples of the development challenges that Dutch disease presented to Latin America's modern economic history.

Given Latin America's comparative advantage in the natural resource sector, it is unrealistic to imagine that these products will cease to have important roles in national economies. Because of such high volatility associated with these natural resources and agricultural products, however, the region has implemented a range of strategies since independence. Most recently, the region has turned somewhat toward fiscal and monetary reforms that use tools like interest and exchange rates to stabilize the economy using a countercyclical approach that counters current economic trends. For most of the twentieth century, Latin American nations sought to diversify production to achieve more stability and development. Capital and durable consumer goods, like appliances or cars, are less susceptible to market changes. It is because of these market realities that social scientists and government leaders in the twentieth and twenty-first centuries have often pushed to create and support Latin American industrial production of capital and durable goods. This objective was easier to achieve for larger countries over the twentieth century, but the share of manufacturing in national economies has increased throughout the region.[11]

Diversifying production also serves as a cushion when markets weaken, or export prices drop. The case of the camera demonstrates this principle, because while capital and durable goods are generally more stable, they are not immune to market fluctuations. Between 1990 and 2010, the camera went from being the hallmark of family vacations to virtually obsolete. Why did the death of the camera not rock national economies? Because those economies producing cameras and related intermediate and consumer products had their eggs in multiple baskets; their economies were diversified. In Latin America, despite diversification proving somewhat successful in domestic markets, the export eggs have historically been split between one, two, or possibly three baskets. In 1870, the leading export averaged half of each country's total export share and the top three export products two-thirds. By 1930, those shares had only increased to 54 and 73 percent, respectively. In Guatemala, Brazil, Cuba, and El Salvador, the leading export represented over 70 percent of all exports. The next four decades saw greater diversification, but the top three exports still represented over half of total exports in 1973.[12]

While diversification and GDP per capita do provide insight into development, they are only a part of the equation. When, for example, resources become disproportionately concentrated in the hands of a few, inequality grows. Most scholars believe that inequality alone is not worrisome, but it becomes problematic when it is consistent and increasing. Latin America's modern era fits the latter growth pattern: growing economies with consistently high and increasing inequality. Over the course of the twentieth century, top income earners saw their share of income increase by 6 percentage points, while the share for bottom income earners decreased by almost 2 percentage points.[13] Much of this inequality grew between 1870 and 1960, and then remained high, but concentrated increases between 1900 and 1929 and World War II and 1960 widened the gap between rich and poor.

The scale of consistent wealth consolidation in Latin America shows that economic growth has resulted in underdevelopment. One way that scholars measure inequality is by calculating the *difference between perfect wealth and actual wealth distribution.* Perfect equality, where everyone has the exact same amount of wealth, is not realistic, *but the degree to which a country deviates from that perfect distribution gives a number between 0 and 1* called the **Gini coefficient**. The closer to zero means the closer to perfect equality, while the closer to one means the more unequal the distribution. Beyond sub-Saharan Africa, Latin America, as a region, has the highest Gini coefficients in the world, in terms of both land and income measures. Practically speaking, this means that the richest 10 percent of each country's population controls around 40 percent of the national wealth, while the poorest 40 percent controls less than 15 percent.[14] These high inequality figures are striking, especially considering that at the start of the nineteenth century, Latin American inequality measures were similar to those for Western Europe. Furthermore, since World War II, and particularly during the 1960s and 1970s, while other regions saw improved wealth distribution, Latin America continued to see increasing inequality.

Broader development indicators also suggest the region's underdevelopment and unequal access to gains and opportunities. In 2019, Latin America's HDI index was 0.766, a number similar to China's. As a region, the index was lower than that for Europe and Central Asia, but higher than indices for East Asia and the Pacific, the Arab States, South Asia, and sub-Saharan Africa. There was, however, a fair degree of variation between countries within the region. In 2022, Southern Cone countries, Costa Rica, and Panama were characterized as having very high human development indices (above 0.898). Latin America's large economies of Brazil and Mexico, alongside Cuba, Peru, Colombia, Ecuador, Dominican Republic, Paraguay, and Bolivia ranked as highly developed (between 0.898 and 0.753). The Central American countries of El Salvador, Guatemala, Nicaragua, and Honduras ranked as medium developed countries (between

0.753 and 0.631), and Haiti was classified as a nation with low development (below 0.513).[15]

A historical HDI for 1900 to 2010 estimates Latin America's average was just 0.18 in 1900. By the middle of the twentieth century, that number would double, and by 2010 it reached an estimated 0.675. These increasing numbers are promising and suggest that from independence through the modern era, for the most part, the trend in Latin America has been toward reduced poverty rates, increasing life expectancy, and higher educational achievements.[16] The 1940s and 1950s represented the greatest relative regional gains in terms of health and education. Figure 1.3 presents a different story. When using the augmented human development index (AHDI) that also considers civil and political liberties alongside other HDI indicators, the 1950–1980 period demonstrates a loss relative to other countries. The figure also shows that Latin America remained below the global AHDI average until 1990, and that the region made minimal gains relative to the rest of the world and to the Western offshoots (Canada, the United States, and Australia). The region's performance relative to East Asia was particularly lackluster. Latin America had a considerable

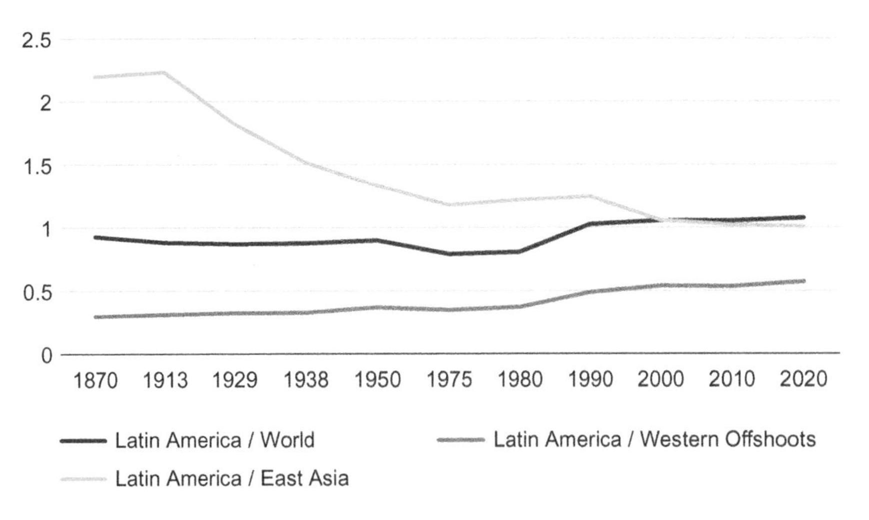

Figure 1.3 Latin America augmented human development index (AHDI) relative to the world and other regions, 1870–2020. Graph elaborated from data in Leandro Prados de la Escosura, "Augmented Human Development in the Age of Globalisation."

Notes: Latin America does not include the British and Dutch Caribbean. AHDI indicators only become available after 1913 for the following countries: Costa Rica, El Salvador, Guatemala, Honduras, and Nicaragua. Indicators are only available after 1950 for the following countries: Dominican Republic, Haiti, Panama, and Paraguay. Western offshoots include the United States, Canada, and Australia. East Asia includes China, Hong Kong, Japan, Macau, Mongolia, North Korea, South Korea, and Taiwan.

advantage of the latter in 1870, but that advantage eroded over the next century and East Asia's AHDI surpassed Latin America's at the turn of the twenty-first century.

Further complicating a discussion of Latin America's development is the fact that welfare gains have hardly been equal across populations. Education provides a good example. While spending on education, primary school enrollments, and literacy rates improved considerably in the twentieth century, concentrated spending in universities rather than primary schools and relatively minimal headway to improve average years of schooling put Latin American countries well behind other countries with similar-sized economies.[17] In fact, "In fourteen republics, more than 40 percent of the labor force had fewer than three years of schooling by 1970."[18]

An additional word of caution is necessary in terms of interpreting this historical HDI. Consistent, reliable data for HDI indicators and much economic data in many Latin American countries only exist after the mid-twentieth century (see the Economic Commission on Latin America – ECLA – in Chapter 5). It can be particularly difficult to find even population data for smaller countries. Thus, scholars interested in historical development must be willing to look to complementary, local statistics on mortality rates, literacy, elementary enrollments, and attendance records for a more nuanced understanding of specific development limits and achievements accompanying modern Latin America's economic growth. When possible, seeing how individual characteristics like gender, race, class, and ethnicity impact these metrics will provide a more robust view of historical development. They can reveal whether certain groups had privileged access to development advancements while others were largely excluded. There is much room to expand research in these areas in future years.

Given these challenges, this book will consider Latin American development from several angles, particularly for the period prior to 1950. Increased production and diversification will be important indicators, but so too will discussions of the growth of elementary education. Health records and standards will complement GDP figures, speaking to quality of life. Infant mortality and life expectancy records provide some insight, but so too can evidence on changes in average heights over time. Anthropometric data have a complicated legacy, as height, weight, and skull size evidence were historically collected to support faulty eugenicist logic. While some pseudo-scientists used the evidence to espouse an ideology of superior and inferior races, changes in heights often reveal people's access to a balanced, nutritional diet, particularly during childhood. Thus, when a group of people, on average, got shorter, an effect called stunting, the decline was most often a result of hardship of some kind, bringing insight to the distribution of opportunities within countries. Combining these various growth and development indicators provides a more holistic understanding of the region's economic history.

Time Periods and Structure

This book divides Latin America's modern economic history into five time periods: 1804–1870; 1870–1930; 1930–1980; 1980–2008; and 2008–2022. The periods coincide with major global economic crises: the Global 1873 Depression in Europe, the Great Depression, the 1980s recession, and the 2008 financial crisis. While other political and economic events shaped the region, these four marked decided changes in the direction of economic history. Analysis of policies and economic data helps define these chronological periods. These data span from evidence on population growth and production figures to a count of constitutional crises and estimates of school enrollment. The correlation of these figures with growth and development is the story of modern Latin American economic history.

The first two periods correspond with the first set of country groups previously described (Table 1.1) and begins with the Independence wars and movements. By 1830, mainland Latin America and Haiti had gained independence, but political instability and economic volatility persisted. Most new nations grappled with European threats and attempts at reinvasion and infighting that stemmed from colonial inequities and power disputes. For the second period, from 1870–1930, most, but not all, of the region was decidedly more stable. Economically, production accelerated as population expanded both naturally and via immigration; new technologies and infrastructure allowed for hinterland expansion; and export and domestic markets increased in an era of global trade. However, this period of economic expansion did not occur without growing pains, and World War I exacerbated existing inequalities and social cleavages for the vast majority of Latin America's population. Rural, Indigenous, and Afro-descended populations were often further marginalized either explicitly or through structural inequities.

The later periods correspond to the second set of country groups (Figure 1.1). By 1930, continued economic disappointment and considerable social unrest, combined with the Great Depression, ushered in a new era. From 1930 to 1979 state-led growth meant that politicians and bureaucrats took a considerably more active role in the economy. Economists were also increasingly included in these conversations, although their advice was not always heeded. The move toward state intervention saw increased industrial and more diversified agricultural production, but national debts also grew. For the population at large, questions of land distribution and education were central issues, as were the pains that came with urbanization and internal migration. The increasing importance of the population's political voice required politicians to engage popular concerns. Effective solutions, however, were hard to find and those that challenged land tenure and the elite's status quo often met with considerable political and social backlash. The Cuban Revolution in 1959 marked a watershed within this period. In the preceding years, proto-populist and populist politicians turned toward expanding production in industrial sectors, aiming to reduce the region's dependence on imports. In the years that followed the Cuban Revolution, it was often authoritarian governments, mostly right-wing, but also on the left, that dictated the terms of state growth.

The global oil crises of the 1970s and economic downturn in the 1980s tested these heavily indebted regimes, bringing scrutiny to human rights violations under authoritarian control and ushering in a new period of market-led growth. From 1980 to 2008, demands of international lenders as well as the inflationary and budgetary challenges of sustained state involvement shrunk the state's role in the national economy. While not a full about-face, a move toward more integrated markets shaped national economic trajectories. Production and growth expanded, and the region made some gains in reducing inequality. By 2008, when the global financial crisis rocked economies across the world, the precarious situation of many Latin Americans brought in a new era of leftist leaders willing to expand the welfare state. This resulting shift has often been referred to as a pink tide. In the years that followed, there was considerable pushback to this movement, leading to a considerable seesaw between Latin America's right and left.

The five defined time periods reflect important shifts, but the changes were rarely completely abrupt. Rather, major events can cause more fringe ideas to come to the fore, accelerating a process of gradual change. Given that change is a process, alternate breaking points could be considered. The middle of the nineteenth century represents one such alternate breaking point. At this time liberal political reformers registered significant gains against conservative counterparts (see **Cinco de Mayo** in Chapter 2). The Catholic Church's role was curtailed, but economically speaking, credit opportunities opened for large ventures. The year 1850 also saw the effective abolition of the transatlantic slave trade, moving the region even closer to a wage labor system. World War I is another alternate break point. Many of the challenges brought to light with the Great Depression and more intentional state intervention in production had their nascent stages in the years following World War I.[19] During the state-led period (1930–1979), 1959 is a considerable turning point with the Cuban Revolution (see Chapter 5). After the island turned toward Soviet-style collectivism, shifts in international lending to the region and political economies influenced the scale of state intervention and indebtedness. For more recent history, while the 2008 financial crisis had a substantial impact on the region, future historians may argue that the 2020 pandemic actually marked the start of a new period. Only time will tell.

Book Structure and Guide

In keeping with the idea of turning points, this book is structured around events that either represented a particular moment in Latin American economic history or that served as mini-turning points in the region. Each introduces the reader to a topic of interest to economic historians. Oftentimes, a particular theme will resurface in other sections. Even if it does not, however, the issue rarely disappears entirely. The 17 events presented in this text cannot cover each individual country. Instead, careful consideration has been given to the geographic distribution and to representing small, medium, and large economies. Equitable geographic distribution can be difficult to achieve because much more has been written on the economic history of Argentina, Brazil, Chile, Colombia, Cuba, Mexico, and Uruguay than for countries like Ecuador, El Salvador, Nicaragua, and Panama. In the very earliest part of the period, some of these countries did not even exist.[20] Nevertheless, sections like Haiti's indemnity payment (Chapter 2), the Peru General Strike (Chapter 4), and discussions of the ECLA (Chapter 5) make explicit efforts to engage smaller countries and the different country subgroups defined in Table 1.1 and Figure 1.1.

In addition to the timeline of events, each chapter contains an accompanying select resource list and bibliography. These should be considered an invitation for deeper analysis into the themes and trajectories outlined in the chapters. A combination of literature and media resources (films, websites, podcasts, etc.) accompany a more traditional secondary source list. Taken together, these resources provide the bridge between macroeconomic events and economic history and the daily lives and cultural production reflecting those realities.

Bibliographic Essay

Within the region, the Latin American Congress of Economic History (CLADHE) hosted its seventh annual conference in Lima, Peru in 2022, and the Economic Commission of Latin American and the Caribbean (ECLAC) serves as a center for research and policy, collecting and divulging up-to-date economic, social, and environmental data. The *Revista de Historia Económica – Journal of Iberian and Latin American History* published three times annually offers robust and nuanced articles related to the region. Articles related to economic history can also be found in national publications like *Revista Uruguaya de História Económica* (Uruguay), *Estudos Econômicos* (Brazil), *Estudios Económicos* (Mexico), and *Tiempo & Economía* (Colombia). Edited volumes and longer introductions to the region's modern economic history are also available. Contributors include both Latin American and foreign scholars, but these regional compilations are most often published in English.

Several of these more extensive introductions to Latin American economic history merit mention as they can provide more detailed explanations of regional variances. Bértola and Ocampo's *The Economic Development of Latin America since Independence* (2012) brings an economic lens to the region's history. It is the most succinct of these compilations as quantitative evidence and statistical data feature more prominently in the text, but the prose is still approachable. Victor Bulmer-Thomas's *Economic History of Latin America since Independence* privileges a narrative approach to the region's economic history. Now in its third edition (2014), the Bulmer-Thomas text demonstrates the continuity between periods. Both studies provide useful appendices with data related to economic growth and development compiled for each country. The two-volume *Cambridge Economic History of Latin America* provides readers with an introduction to specific topics ranging from fiscal and monetary regimes to labor and immigration. The first volume combines the colonial period through 1870, while the second covers the long twentieth century, which ran from 1870 to 2000. As an edited volume, it provides a good starting point for more specific questions. Enrique Cárdenas, José Antonio Ocampo, and Rosemary Thorp also edited a three-volume *An Economic History of Twentieth-Century Latin America* that is particularly insightful for the export-led and state-led growth periods.[21] Each of these works in some way addresses development shortcomings, but Latin American economic growth challenges and successes take primacy. These texts often struggle to make explicit connections to daily lives, leaving readers to speculate how something like a national balance of payment imbalance impacts the types of jobs available or how a food shortage's impact on households and individuals translates into cultural patterns and artistic movements.

Several other edited volumes explore economic themes for more nuanced topics from historical immigration to inequality. Many are geared towards economics students and researchers, bringing together leading scholars to provide useful data and insightful analyses. Some of these, like Bértola and Williamson's *Has Latin American Inequality Changed Direction* (2017), Williamson's *Five Centuries of Latin American Income Inequality* (2009), and Camou, Maubrigades, and Thorp's *Gender Inequalities and Development in Latin America during the Twentieth Century* (2017), prioritize topics more closely related to the human development index and varied development experiences. For a more historical approach to the region, scholars will find that Topik, Marichal, and Frank's *From Silver to Cocaine: Latin American Commodity Chains and the Building of the World Economy, 1500–2000* (2006) provides an approachable analysis where coffee, henequen, and export products take center stage. In each of these studies discussions of daily lives are few and far between. In *Latin American Labor Organizations*, editors Greenfield and Maram (1987) get closer to these realities, with scholars providing a comprehensive listing of labor organizations country by country. Finally, to find a deeper set of resources written prior to the 1980s readers should consult Cortés-Condé and Stein's *Latin America: A Guide to Economic History 1850–1930* (1977). Contributors provided extensive bibliographic essays for each country based on a range of topics, including but not limited to demography, structures and institutions, agriculture, industry, and transportation.

Notes

1 Robert McKee Irwin, Maricruz Castro, Mónica Szurmuk, Inmaculada Gordillo Alvarez, and Dubravka Suznjevic. *Global Mexican Cinema: Its Golden Age*. London: Palgrave Macmillan, 2013.
2 Bulmer-Thomas, *Economic History of Latin America*, utilizes the Latin America six. Much more data are available for these countries, which lend to their prominence in scholarly studies. Bértola and Ocampo finetune these divisions in their survey *The Economic Development of Latin America since Independence*.
3 Engerman and Sokoloff, "Factor Endowments," propose that the region's natural endowments of labor, soil type, and mining sector were key in shaping modern economic history (see theories in this chapter).
4 "Volume and direction of the trans-Atlantic slave trade" map 9 from slavevoyages.org. Estimates include Dutch Caribbean and South America.
5 Puerto Rico and Cuba were still Spanish colonies until the Spanish-American War in 1898. Following the Spanish defeat, Cuba gained independence, while Puerto Rico was made into a protectorate of the United States and remains so today.
6 Tropical agriculture was an important part of Costa Rica's nineteenth-century export economy, but European-descended populations were the dominant labor force.
7 The index runs between 0, which is the least developed, and 1, which is the most developed. For life expectancy, 85 years receives a 1, 20 a 0. For income, $75,000 GNI per capita is a 1 and $100 is a 0. Schooling considers the average of mean years of schooling and expected years of schooling, with 15 years and 18 representing 1.
8 The augmented human development index (AHDI) developed by Leandro Prados de la Escosura, "Augmented Human Development," does include a liberty index in its calculation.
9 GDP increased 140-fold during the period. Bértola and Ocampo, *Economic Development*, table 1.1. Population increased from 22 million in 1820 to 580 million in 2008.
10 This definition of commodity does not extend to the concepts of commodification, which explores the process by which cultural practices are assigned an exchange value.
11 Mitchell, *International Historical Statistics: the Americas*, pp. 305–9.
12 Bértola and Ocampo, *Economic History*, table 1.7, p. 22.

13 Astorga, "The Haves and the Have-Nots," table 1.
14 Bulmer-Thomas, *Economic History of Latin America*, 2nd edition, table 1.5.
15 Based on the United Nations Human Development Index: https://hdr.undp.org/data-center/human-development-index#/indicies/HDI, accessed January 2024. Norway has the highest HDI at 0.957. The United States' HDI is 0.926.
16 Bulmer-Thomas, *Economic History of Latin America*, 3rd edition, p. 332, shows that only in Haiti did living standards between 1950 and 1970 regress.
17 United Nations, *Anuario estadístico*, 31 and 57.
18 Bulmer-Thomas, *Economic History of Latin America*, 3rd edition, p. 337.
19 Bulmer-Thomas's *Economic History of Latin America* uses 1850 and 1914 as break points.
20 It was not until the late 1830s that the United Provinces of Central America splintered, and 1830 and 1903, respectively, that Ecuador and Panama "separated" from the Republic of Colombia, the latter with significant assistance from the United States, who was keen on developing the Panama Canal.
21 This three-volume work followed Rosemary Thorp's *Progress, Poverty, and Exclusion: An Economic History of Latin America in the Twentieth Century*.

Suggested Media, Literature, and Digital Resources

Buñuel, Luis, Oscar Dancigers, Luis Alcoriza, et al. *Los Olvidados / The Young and the Damned*. México: Televisa S.A. de C.V., 2004.
United Nations. "United Nations: ECLAC." Accessed September 13, 2023. https://www.cepal.org/en.
University of Groningen. "Maddison Project Database." 2020. https://www.rug.nl/ggdc/historicaldevelopment/maddison/.

Select Bibliography

Acemoglu, Daron, Simon Johnson, and James A. Robinson. "The Colonial Origins of Comparative Development: An Empirical Investigation." *American Economic Review* 91, no. 5 (2001): 1369–1401.
Astorga, Pablo Junquera. "The Haves and the Have-Nots in Latin America in the 20th Century." *Revista de Economía Mundial* 43 (2016): 47–68.
Astorga, Pablo, Ame R. Bergés, and Valpy Fitzgerald. "Productivity Growth in Latin America over the Long Run." *Review of Income and Wealth* 57, no. 2 (2011): 203–23.
Bértola, Luis, and José Antonio Ocampo. *The Economic Development of Latin America since Independence*. Oxford: Oxford University Press, 2012.
Bértola, Luis, and Jeffrey G. Williamson, eds. *Has Latin American Inequality Changed Direction? Looking over the Long Run*. Cham, Switzerland: Springer Open, 2017.
Bolt, Jutta, and Jan Luiten Van Zanden. "The Maddison Project: Collaborative Research on Historical National Accounts." *The Economic History Review* 67, no. 3 (2014): 627–51. http://www.jstor.org/stable/42921771.
Bulmer-Thomas, Victor. *The Economic History of Latin America since Independence*, Second edition. New York: Cambridge University Press, 2003.
Bulmer-Thomas, Victor. *The Economic History of Latin America since Independence*, Third edition. New York: Cambridge University Press, 2014.
Bulmer-Thomas, Victor, John H. Coatsworth, and Roberto Cortés Conde, eds. *The Cambridge Economic History of Latin America*, 2 volumes. New York: Cambridge University Press, 2006.

Camou, Maria Magdalena, Silvana Maubrigades, and Rosemary Thorp. *Gender Inequalities and Development in Latin America during the Twentieth Century*. London: Routledge, 2016. https://doi.org/10.4324/9781315584041.

Cárdenas, Enrique, Jose Ocampo, and Rosemary Thorp, eds. *An Economic History of Twentieth-Century Latin America: Volume 3: Industrialization and the State in Latin America: The Postwar Years*. London: Palgrave Macmillan, 2000.

Cortes Conde, Roberto, Stanley J. Stein, Jirina Rybacek-Mlynkova, and Jiřina Rybáček-Mlýnková. *Latin America: A Guide to Economic History, 1830–1930*. Berkeley: University of California Press, 1977.

Engerman, Stanley L., and Kenneth L. Sokoloff. "Factor Endowments, Institutions, and Differential Paths of Growth among New World Economics." In *How Latin America Fell Behind*, edited by Stephen H. Haber, 260–304. Stanford: Stanford University Press, 1997.

Frankema, Ewout. *Has Latin America Always Been Unequal? A Comparative Study of Asset and Income Inequality in the Long Twentieth Century*. Leiden: Brill, 2009.

Greenfield, Gerald Michael, and Sheldon L. Maram. *Latin American Labor Organizations*. New York: Greenwood Press, 1987.

Haber, Stephen H. *How Latin America Fell Behind: Essays on the Economic Histories of Brazil and Mexico, 1800–1914*. Stanford: Stanford University Press, 1997.

Mitchell, Brian R. *International Historical Statistics: the Americas, 1750–1993*. London: Macmillan, 1998.

Palma, José Gabriel. "De-industrialisation, 'Premature' De-industrialisation and the Dutch Disease." *Revista NECAT-Revista do Núcleo de Estudos de Economia Catarinense* 3, no. 5 (2014): 7–23.

Prados de la Escosura, Leandro. "Augmented Human Development in the Age of Globalization." *The Economic History Review* 74, no. 4 (2021): 946–75.

———. "Inequality and Poverty in Latin America: A Long-Run Exploration." In *The New Comparative Economic History: Essays in Honor of Jeffrey G. Williamson*, edited by Timothy J. Hatton, Kevin H. O'Rourke, and Alan M. Taylor, chap. 12. Cambridge: MIT Press.

Thorp, Rosemary. *Progress, Poverty and Exclusion: An Economic History of Latin America in the Twentieth Century*. Baltimore: Johns Hopkins Press, 1998.

Topik, Steven, Carlos Marichal, and Zephyr L. Frank. *From Silver to Cocaine: Latin American Commodity Chains and the Building of the World Economy, 1500–2000*. Durham: Duke University Press, 2006.

United Nations. Economic Commission for Latin America and the Caribbean. *Anuario estadístico de América Latina y el Caribe*. Santiago: ECLAC, 1990.

Williamson, Jeffrey G. "Five Centuries of Latin American Income Inequality." *Revista de Historia Económica* 28, no. 2 (2010): 227–52. https://doi.org/10.1017/S0212610910000078.

2 New Nations (Independence–1870)

The first era of modern Latin American economic history came in the wake of independence movements and struggles. During the mid-eighteenth century, a series of reforms known as the Bourbon and Pombaline Reforms brought dramatic economic, geographic, and social reforms to Latin America's Spanish and Portuguese colonies, respectively. The metropolises, embroiled in continental wars that required heavy spending, looked to Latin America as a partial solution. Silver, gold, and diamond deposits and nutrient-rich soil where sugar production thrived were traditional goods exported to the metropolis, but the reforms saw expanded internal and foreign trade and a diversification of production into other agricultural sectors. The reforms also increased taxes for those living in Latin America. The region, however, saw little of this increased tax burden reinvested in the vast continent. Even the roads meant to transport these goods so valuable to Spain and Portugal remained woefully maintained. The Bourbon and Pombaline Reforms also reified and even strengthened elite hierarchies, putting individuals born in Europe at the top. Any enthusiasm for the reforms was increasingly challenged by creole, American-born, elites.

The reforms also exacerbated tensions among the general population. In the Andean region, partly Indigenous leader José Gabriel Condorcanqui, also known as Túpac Amaru, his Afro-Indigenous wife Micaela Bastides, Tomás Katari, and Julián Apaza led a multi-class and multi-racial revolt against increasing taxes, bad government, and the colonial status quo in 1780. Although swiftly defeated, the fact that over 11,000 joined their cause within days demonstrated mass discontent. Known as the Great Rebellion, it was far from the only revolt; throughout Latin America, general discontent saw an increase in rebellions and revolts in the wake of the Bourbon and Pombaline Reforms. Up until 1781, the Great Rebellion was the most prominent display of discontent.

The next major rebellion came from neither a Spanish nor Portuguese colony, but rather from the French colony of St. Domingue, present-day Haiti. Between 1783 and 1791, St. Domingue received one-third of the

DOI: 10.4324/9781003283843-2

Atlantic slave trade, and by 1789, most inhabitants were African-born. This population included an increasing maroon population made up of enslaved individuals who had deserted their plantations and settled in the surrounding hinterlands. In August 1791, following a religious ceremony in Bois Caiman, a mass slave rebellion began. Their rebellion transformed into the Haitian Revolution, as Haiti proclaimed its independence in 1804. Yet, recognition of that independence with the **1825 Agreement** proved incredibly costly to the new country.

Less than 30 years after Haitian independence, all of mainland Latin America was independent from Europe.[1] The years that followed represented a pivotal period in the region's modern economic history, one in which recolonization threats, crippling debt payments, and heavy regional infighting left few funds for social services and challenged the region's ability to develop to its full potential. When any stability was established, export economies were prioritized, with railways like the **Güines Railroad** in Cuba taking center stage. Internal political instability also crippled the region as liberals pushed conservatives toward measures that would make land a tradable asset, theoretically expand public education, and weaken the Catholic Church's connection to the State. Liberal reforms became the regional standard by 1860, but they were not always popular, as demonstrated by the French Intervention and Mexico's **Cinco de Mayo**, a battle in which Mexicans defeated the French forces. States struggled to adequately fund education and other public works projects and many Catholics in the region saw the reforms as unfairly targeting the Catholic Church. Thus, as civil and regional conflict continued, Latin America's development suffered. The region's resources made it arguably better off than the United States and Canada at the end of the colonial period, but by 1870, Latin America had fallen behind.

1825 Agreement (Port-au-Prince, Haiti)

In 1825, amidst a blockade and under the threat of French invasion and re-enslavement, Haiti agreed to repay 150 million francs to France. The terms of the **1825 Agreement** were steep for the new nation and left little room for development spending. In many ways, Haiti is still repaying this debt. This event demonstrates the impact of sovereign debt to American nations in their infancy: national debt could be crippling. As nascent nations, Latin American countries had to find revenues and decide where they were going to spend money. With heavy military and debt payments, there was little left for infrastructure and public works investments. Furthermore, the 1825 Agreement, in particular, demonstrates the long-term impact that historic events can make on a country's development.

As Latin America transitioned from independence movements to nation building, leaders looked not only to secure, but also to finance, their new nations. As colonies, the region's export economies centered around precious metals and sugar, and local economies developed to complement these enterprises. Independence wars, however, wreaked havoc in many places and most of the new nations – with the exception of Brazil, an empire, and Cuba and Puerto Rico, still colonies – had just spent years fighting their largest trading partner. Furthermore, attempts from colonial powers to recolonize continued, meaning the majority of national budgets were justifiably allocated toward military expenditures. Expenses outpaced revenues and these countries operated at considerable deficits, spending more than they received. Nowhere was this predicament more acute than in Haiti, the region's first independent nation.

As French Saint Domingue, Haiti was the world's richest colony, known as the "Jewel of the Antilles." It produced coffee, rum, cotton, and indigo, but sugar was its most lucrative crop. By 1789, 75 percent of the world's sugar came from Saint Domingue, but the backbreaking labor was predominantly performed by enslaved individuals. By 1791, 90 percent of Saint Domingue's population was Black or Afro-descended, 80 percent was enslaved, and half had been born on the African continent. In that year, a massive, coordinated slave rebellion sent St. Domingue into a 13-year fight for independence. That prolonged fight included France's abolishment of slavery in an effort to retain the colony; the proposed re-enslavement of the population by Napoleon; and massacres of the surviving French population ordered by the Black general Dessalines. The chaos left the entire region terrified of a similar uprising. The fear was so great that Haiti was left isolated diplomatically and economically.

Independence was claimed in 1804, but competing states and ideologies governed the north and south and the sides only united in 1818. Unity did not bring recognition, as France and most other European nations refused to recognize Haiti's sovereignty.[2] (The United States' recognition of Haitian independence only came after the Emancipation Proclamation in 1863.) Exiled colonists tried to convince the king of France, Louis XVIII, to reconquer the island, reimpose slavery, and re-institute the slave trade. When recognition finally came, it was at an exorbitant price. Under a tour de force that included 14 warships docked in Port-au-Prince harbor and the threat of French reinvasion, Haiti's then President for Life, General Boyer, accepted the humiliating terms. In addition to French ships only paying half of the docking fees of other nations, Haiti would be liable for an indemnity payment: 150 million francs to former slave owners for compensation of lost property both human and physical. It was an exorbitant sum that was five times France's total annual budget.

In a country where much of the land had been ravished by the Revolution, timely payments were impossible. Exacerbating the issue was the outlay of military costs to sustain independence and to bring independence to Spanish Santo Domingo. In 1822, the former Spanish colony on the eastern side of the island of Hispaniola began organizing an independence movement. Boyer and the Haitian army joined the cause and Santo Domingo gained independence from Spain. Independence brought abolition and Santo Domingo was "voluntarily incorporated to the Haitian Republic."[3] Dominicans, however, came to see unification as synonymous with Boyer's oppression and higher taxes, and moved toward separation from the Republic. Discontent regarding suppression of Spanish cultural practices and language was restricted to the Dominican side of the island, but inhabitants on both sides of Hispaniola complained about taxes.

Boyer nationalized the debt, making all Haitians now responsible for its payment, including those Dominicans in eastern Hispaniola. The population suffered under the new taxes to pay the debt; overproduction of agricultural products led to erosion and stripped the land; and printing money increased inflation, which made everyday items more expensive. Haiti took out loans with interest from French banks to pay, defaulted on several payments, and tried to renegotiate the terms in what became known as a "double debt." In 1838 a new treaty reduced the payment to 60 million francs, but it was a debt that would not be paid off until 1910. When it was all said and done, Haiti had borrowed over 166 million francs to pay the 60-million-franc debt, with over half of the payments going to French, European, and later on, US banks for fees and interest. Making these payments left little for investing in development.

For the population at large, the decision to nationalize debt equated to a daily life still dominated by agriculture. Boyer's 1826 Rural Code prioritized large-scale farms to be able to meet debt payments and criminalized vagrancy to ensure that there were enough workers for agriculture. Enforcement was inconsistent, and many peasants turned to small-scale agricultural labor. No matter where they were, the crippling debt payments impacted everyone. Haiti used metal-backed currency, currency with a percentage of gold or silver, to ensure its value, to pay down debts. Left with minimal specie after paying these debts, Haiti adopted a paper currency, and increased printing through 1860 led to inflation. Paying 16 (Haitian gourdes) for a single chicken and similarly high prices for vegetables most impacted the budgets of the lower class.[4] Increasing inflation also made planning for the future risky: why save when there was no guarantee that your money would have value in the future? Exacerbating the issues was that the country's revenues were particularly susceptible to global fluctuations in coffee prices, the main export revenue. Southern estate owners revolted in 1843, and overthrew Boyer, but shortly thereafter, a more popular uprising from the region threatened elite merchant and military political rule that followed. Known as the Piquet movement, it was led by Jean-Jacques Accau, an agriculturalist and former member of the rural police. Adherents advocated for land reform, national education, and higher prices awarded to peasant farmers for their crops. The demands were understandable, but the national debt burden prevented a full discussion, and concessions ultimately quelled the uprising. The eastern side of Hispaniola also revolted, and the Dominican Republic claimed its separate independence in 1844, marking a tense divide on the island that persists today.

Other new nations in Latin America did not suffer crippling debt payments to the scale of Haiti, but the logistical challenges of nation building in the wake of independence battles were still considerable. This meant that leaders in the 1820s often looked externally for funding. By 1825, the same year that Haiti signed the indemnity agreement, Colombia, Chile, Peru, Argentina, Brazil, Mexico, and Central America all *issued government bonds to try and raise money for the new nations. Investors bought the bonds on the capital markets* in London and Amsterdam, *looking forward to repayments with interest*, increasing the region's **sovereign debt**. As a region, Latin America accounted for one-third of total investment on the Royal Exchange in London. But, as their outside debts increased, so too did the challenges of keeping together these young nations: infighting was prevalent as regional leaders jockeyed for power. Internal conflicts persisted for most of the former Spanish colonies, with 20 different constitutions forming between 1820 and 1829. As governments entered into crises, debt repayments lagged. By 1827, the riskiness of the Latin American bonds was apparent to outside investors as every government bond issued by Latin American nations had not been fully paid and was in default.

With external lenders wary of default, and old tax systems abolished, leaders looked for other revenues. Diversifying production with new agricultural products and natural resources proved somewhat lucrative, especially from 1850 to 1875, even though traditional colonial exports had lackluster performances in the wake of independence. In Haiti, coffee, cotton, and logwoods took center stage; coffee became central to Brazil and important in Costa Rica and Colombia; cacao production expanded substantially in Ecuador and Colombia; and cattle and cattle byproducts expanded in Argentina. Taxing trade, both exports and imports, covered most national deficits for Chile and Brazil and provided some relief across the region. However, despite these shifts, export growth was muted and the growth in export revenues only increased by 2.2 percent annually, less than half the 4.7 percent annual rate in the United States. Wherever there had been battles and fighting, what infrastructure had been present had often been damaged: mines had been destroyed and fields had been burned.[5] With the exception of Peru's guano boom in the 1850s and '60s, it was *taxes levied on imported goods* that supplied 80–90 percent of trade taxes to governments. As these **import tariffs** were passed onto consumers in the form of higher prices, it meant increased costs of finished consumer products like textiles and wines and increased costs to innovate in agriculture and industrial production.

Leaders also looked internally for new sources of revenue, particularly for state and provincial funding needs. The non-export economy, after all, was much larger than the export market, as daily interactions, artisan-built products, construction, domestic service, and transactions in marketplaces, across towns and provinces dominated everyday experiences and monetary exchanges. Countries tried to harness this potential. New taxes on trade between provinces, internal sales and transit taxes, provided most of the provincial and state revenues in every country but Chile and Brazil. These new sources of revenue, however, made trade between provinces and states more costly and the pace of internal market development was slower than external market development. Mexico, for example, introduced a tax on pulque, a popular pre-colonial fermented beverage from agave. But pulque was largely consumed by Mexico's Indigenous and mestizo populations; thus, groups marginalized in the hierarchical social structure were also targeted economically with these new taxes. The rise in costs of basic needs associated with the internal sales and transit taxes would also have proved a greater burden on the majority rather than elites. Ultimately, economic changes did little to challenge enduring social structures that rewarded social connections and discriminated against the region's poor populations, many of whom were Indigenous, Black, or of mixed descent.

How were national budgets allocated? In general, over 50 percent of the new countries' budgets went to the military, and during periods of intense strife, the share increased to upwards of 70 percent. Death and conflict did not stop with independence. In Haiti, for example, military campaigns to retain Santo Domingo, the former Spanish colony on the eastern side of the island, required investment. So too did the threat of reinvasion from France, a plausible threat given continued European incursions in the region well after independence (see Figure 2.1). Not only was 25 percent of Haiti's adult male population employed in the military or national guard, but revenues not being directed toward indemnity payments often went to the military. In 1837, military spending accounted for 60 percent of Haiti's budget. These commitments left very little for investments in infrastructure, education, and other services. As one diplomat noted of the streets in the capital in 1866, "They have once been paved, and now neglected, and are now more rough and uneven than if they had never been paved at all."[6] It would not be until 1860 that the Haitian economy would grow. Only after the standing military was reduced to half its size, quality

Figure 2.1 The Spanish bombarding Peru's principal port, Callao, in March 1866. The attack followed a similar one on Valparaíso in Chile. The threat of European invasion well into the nineteenth century helped keep Latin American military budgets high. *Bombardment of Callao, May 2*. Callao Bay Peru, 1868. Photograph. Library of Congress, LC-USZ62-136429.

controls on exports were implemented, and the printing of paper currency was limited did investments in infrastructure, free schools, and services become feasible.

Brazil, by far the most stable nation in the region, was the only country to resolve its debts in a timely fashion, so it was able to continue to issue foreign debt, but the creditworthiness of other nations was questionable at best.[7] The hemispheric defaults led foreign investors largely to stay away from Latin America until the middle of the nineteenth century. Around the 1850s, while Central America, Ecuador, and Bolivia remained politically unstable, the Southern Cone, Brazil, and Cuba (still a Spanish colony) achieved relative stability. This brought a second round of loans issued to those more stable countries between 1850 and 1875. Nations not only secured loans for refinancing existing loans in arrears, but finally began investing in public works projects. Whereas 68 percent of the nine loans issued to the region in the 1850s were directed toward refinancing past debts and 32 percent toward public works, the ratio had flipped by the 1870s, with 60 percent of the 22 loans directed toward public works projects, predominantly railroad construction and port modernization.

Güines Railroad Opens in Cuba, 1837 (Havana, Cuba)

On November 19, 1837, the first railroad in Latin America opened, linking Bejucal to Havana, Cuba. Construction began in 1834 and was performed largely by local journeymen, enslaved (including those rented out by their enslavers), and freedmen. The official *Junta de Fomento* and private contractors, mostly from the United States, oversaw the project. Just over 15km of track, the Güines Railroad connected a portion of Cuba's sugar-producing interior to the port of Havana. Creole sugar producers had become tired of "carts broken into pieces, destroyed sugar crates, worn out animals, lost days that drag on and cause incalculable losses to the laborious farmer," challenges they equated with the poor road system.[8] Maintaining traditional roads was costly, required considerable labor, and had yielded subpar results. The Spanish, who still ruled the island, were committed to making Cuban sugar profitable in an increasingly competitive global market. The commitment was such that Spain supported railway construction in their colony nine years before the first tracks would open in the metropolis.[9] By 1870, Cuba, ironically still a colony, accounted for one-quarter of Latin America's railway lines: at just 1,250km long, the island of Cuba had almost 1,300km of railway track. The Güines Railway demonstrates that when governments could, they generally invested in specific types of public services. Despite legislation connecting the state to public provision of education, when funds were available, infrastructure such as railways and ports often took priority. This left Latin America's educational system largely underdeveloped by the end of the period in 1870.

Between 1850 and 1875, a new round of foreign financing became available to Latin American nations. In the 1850s, loans that did not go toward refinancing debt, which constituted 68 percent of loans, were directed toward public works. In the 1860s, despite a rise in military spending, 12 percent of loans still went toward public works. In Argentina, Bolivia, Chile, Costa Rica, Guatemala, Honduras, Paraguay, and the Dominican Republic, over half of all funds secured through loans between 1850 and 1875 was spent on building infrastructure for domestic and external trade, mostly railroads and ports. Latin American geographies challenged transportation: mountains and high plateaus impeded construction, rivers were often unnavigable, or only partially so during certain times of year, and swampy areas and rainy seasons made maintenance nearly impossible. Security was poor on abysmally maintained roads and mules were often the best alternative form of transport as even carts' wheels were unable to reliably traverse trade routes. It was no wonder that countries looked toward railway transport as a welcome boon.

It would take until the 1850s for the first lines in many countries to open. A new round of loans from foreign investors often helped finance these ventures, but construction frequently remained limited through 1870. Colombia opened track on the Panama isthmus in 1855, but by 1870, counted just 55km of rail in service. Brazil inaugurated its first railway in 1854, but the country, over 75 times larger than Cuba, had just over half the railway in service as the small sugar-producing colony by 1870. Varied topographies challenged more extensive expansion, but these early investments would prove profitable in countries able to construct railways. In Peru and Honduras, railway lines failed to materialize as it was corruption and graft, rather than the environment, that eroded construction.

Competing with infrastructure in national budgets were other public goods provisions like sanitation, education, health, justice, and safety. The budgetary commitments ranged between non-existent to minimal. Education offers an instructive example of the trend toward underdevelopment in the region. During the nineteenth century, Latin America fell behind the developed world in terms of average years of schooling. By the end of the century, the average citizen in developed countries had attended school for almost six and a half years, but in Latin America, the typical adult did not even have a full year's school education. In Uruguay, which boasted the highest educational achievement rates, the typical person had received just 2.4 years of schooling, a full four years less than their counterpart in the United States or Western Europe. Systematic education data on this era can be difficult to find, but the mismatch between legislation and educational achievements supports the interpretation that Latin America fell behind throughout the century and not just in the last three decades (a period covered in the next chapter).

Legislatively, nominal support of education appeared in a handful of countries shortly after independence. Peru supported "free primary instruction for all citizens" as early as 1828, Ecuador passed a law of public education in 1835, and Chile passed a similar law in 1833. By 1870, Cuba, Bolivia, Mexico, Costa Rica, and Venezuela had similar laws that expanded public primary education. Even Haiti, saddled with debt payments, opened its Ministry of Public Education in 1843. Transforming these laws and ministries into effective schooling for children often proved impossible during this era. Even in Chile, which was one of the first countries to truly develop a public education infrastructure and system, just 0.4 percent of GDP was spent on public education. In Haiti, between 5 and 10 percent of public revenue was budgeted for schools, but by 1866, just 2.69 percent of the school-aged population was enrolled.[10]

Differences between expenditures and budgets show adequate and consistent funding as a major challenge facing public schools. National, state, provincial, and local governments often left room in their budgets for schools, but actual expenditures did not keep pace. This lack of funding for public schools was not a burden for the elite, who sent their children to private schools, hired tutors, or even sent them to Europe for school. Those who lost out were the sons and daughters of laborers or peasant farmers whose chances for social mobility remained increasingly constrained as Latin America moved toward greater integration into global markets and as manufacturing took root. For young boys and young men, military service continued to be their connection between the state and social mobility. For young girls, social mobility through a favorable marriage remained the best path.

The level of government (state/provincial, municipal, or national) providing educational funding also produced major differences throughout the region. For citizens fortunate to live in countries with an early-developing education system, state/provincial or municipal governments, rather than the national government, were responsible for schools, both in funding and finding appropriate buildings and teachers. Here public schools competed directly for funds with other public services like provisioning municipal slaughterhouses, cemeteries, and markets that became part of hygiene efforts during the era. As such, states/provinces and municipalities with greater resources were better positioned to open and better provision more schools. More marginalized towns or rural populations fared worse. In El Salvador, for example, if municipalities were unable to provide resources for public schools, the burden was passed on to parents. Asked to pay 4 reales per child for attendance, many parents would have been unable to pay this cost.[11] In the case of Mexico, where municipal and state governments financed schools, there was considerable variance between major urban centers and the rest of the country. As early as the 1830s, half the children in the Mexican cities of Guadalajara, Mexico City, and Puebla were enrolled in a combination of private and public schools. In the city of Guadalajara, by 1842 over half of the primary-school-age population was enrolled in municipal schools. In contrast, in the northern and largely rural state of Coahuila, just 10 percent of the school-age population attended schools.

Constrained budgets explained some of the slow public school development, but so too did the significant role the Catholic Church held in the region. During the colonial period, the Catholic Church was the primary educator of Latin American youth. After independence, even though the Church was often associated with conservative royalists, its hold over education did not disappear. In fact, the Catholic Church remained the primary source of education throughout most of the nineteenth century and had the support of many conservatives and average citizens in this role. Liberals, in contrast, generally lobbied for a separation of church and state. Their view for education expanded opportunities not only for poor citizens, but also for women, and became more popular in the mid-nineteenth century. Missing from the educational system, however, were significant enslaved populations in parts of Latin America. Cuba may have expanded education to poor children in 1841, but as they continued to import enslaved individuals this provision excluded the most exploited children until abolition in 1886.

For those schools that did open during the period, the pedagogical model moved toward a more standardized education system and largely followed the Lancaster framework. Instead of general classrooms, students would be divided into schoolyear cohorts. A hallmark of the model was the normal school, an institution dedicated to educating future teachers that remains an important institution in Latin American education in the twenty-first century. The primary goal of this new educational approach was to cultivate new citizens with the technical know-how to propel Latin America forward. Unfortunately, financial constraints, alternate priorities, social norms, and political infighting prevented full enactment of the liberal educational vision.[12]

Measures of national literacy rates and average years of schooling attest to the failure to adequately execute these reforms. In Honduras, adults between the ages of 15 and 64 averaged less than four months of schooling by 1900. The rates in 1870 would have been even lower.[13] There were, however, some winners as public schools developed during the nineteenth century. For the most part, they were school-aged boys living in growing urban centers. Removed from political violence that concentrated in the countryside, taught by educators trained in normal schools, closer to transportation networks, urban centers like Guadalajara in Mexico showed that public schools could be successful.

Cinco de Mayo, 1862 (Puebla, Mexico)

Cinco de Mayo represents two important trends in Latin America's nineteenth-century history. First, it shows the interconnectedness of political instability that left much of Latin America, particularly Spanish America, playing a game of catch-up economically in the nineteenth century. Second, it demonstrates the conflictive and complex role liberal reforms played in the nineteenth century. Not everyone supported liberal reforms, but they did make credit more widely available and expanded production and scale in the region. Nevertheless, access to that credit was still largely restricted to elite sectors of society.

In the United States Cinco de Mayo is the most visible public celebration of Mexican identity and heritage. Its popularity, however, is not because Mexicans celebrate the day with equal fervor; the "holiday" is a byproduct of Mexican immigrants in the United States finding a way to celebrate their history in a way that would prove inoffensive in an era of anti-immigrant sentiment in the 1920s and '30s. Cinco de Mayo celebrates the Mexican armed forces' victory over the French armed forces in the Battle of Puebla in 1862.[14] While the Mexicans won the battle, ultimately they failed to prevent French invasion. The French armed forces, most of whom were colonial subjects from the Caribbean or Africa, occupied Mexico's capital and installed Emperor Maximiliano between 1864 to 1867 with the support of Mexican conservatives. Mexico's ousted liberal President, Benito Juárez, tried to govern, rather unsuccessfully, while on the run, but in 1867, Maximiliano was captured and executed by a firing squad. An important structural change, however, took place under his tenure that would expand Mexico's credit market and open new opportunities for those fortunate to be considered Mexican elite.

Infighting amongst regional strongmen vying for power, known as *caudillos*, left Spanish America splintered into 16 different countries by 1839. Political disputes between conservatives and liberals ushered in new government after new government and new constitution after new constitution from Argentina to Mexico and in every country in between. In Mexico, between 1835 and 1846, there were 18 different executive tenures of 10 different men. In 1848, conflict between the United States and Mexico halted internal disputes. Territorial expansion from the United States and the extension of cotton growing and slavery into Texas and Mexican territories where slavery had been abolished, launched the Mexican-American War, or the *Intervención Estadounidense* as it is known in Mexico. Mexico was unable to sustain the two-front conflict and, in the 1848 Treaty of Guadalupe-Hidalgo, ceded 55 percent of its national lands to the United States. This also ushered in a return to the 1824 Constitution.

Less than ten years later, a new constitution brought out internal infighting between liberals and conservatives, resulting in substantial instability. The 1857 Constitution instituted a number of liberal reforms aimed to increase Mexican agricultural wealth and eliminate **debt peonage**, which had kept *workers indefinitely indebted and bound to landowners until they paid off monetary advancements*. Liberals planned to dismantle existing land structures, which included both the hacienda system that accumulated enormous tracts of land in the hands of the few, and Indigenous communal land-holding practices. Reforms also placed significant limits to the Catholic Church. This last reform was the straw that broke the camel's back for conservatives. Mexico was a country whose first independence struggles were fought under the flag of the Virgin of Guadalupe led by the radical priest Miguel Hidalgo.[15] In other words, it is difficult to exaggerate the staunch religiosity of much of Mexico's population and the pervasive influence of the Church.

Civil conflict erupted, beginning what would become known as the Wars of Reform. After three years of conflict, the Catholic-supporting conservatives were on the losing side. In 1861, President Benito Juárez enacted the 1857 Constitution, but much of the country's infrastructure had been destroyed and Mexico was again unable to pay its foreign debts. By the 1850s Mexico's debts totaled 15 million pesos. Political instability does not make for good debtors and Juárez suspended debt repayments. Most of Mexico's foreign debt payments were going, or rather not going, to the Spanish, British, and French. It was then that Mexican conservatives took a drastic step and approached the French about invading to collect their debts, an invitation that the French accepted. The United States, embroiled in its own civil war, would not intervene, despite France's clear violation of the 1823 **Monroe Doctrine**. The doctrine, which would be used to justify US intervention in the region in future decades, held that *any further European colonial extension in the Americas into nations recognized as independent would also be seen a threat to the United States.*

The inability to pay debts due to political instability was not unique to Mexico. Regional territorial disputes brought some of the greatest conflict and proved the most devastating, particularly to Paraguay and Bolivia. The War of the Triple Alliance, also known as the Paraguay War, lasted from 1864–1870. It pitted Paraguay, led by Francisco Solano López, and Uruguay's *blancos* against Argentina, Brazil, and Uruguay's *colorados*. Ultimately, Paraguay lost significant portions of its national territory, but more importantly, 35 percent of Paraguay's entire population died, including 75 percent of the adult male population.[16] Every Paraguayan male was drafted into the military campaign, leaving under-cultivated crops and the entire population vulnerable to starvation. The War of the Pacific (1879–1883), while technically after the new nation period, similarly left Bolivia reeling. Chile defeated the Peru-Bolivia alliance, extending its Pacific coastline and gaining nitrate-rich territory. Chile's gain, however, came at a tremendous cost to Bolivia's development. Already facing transportation challenges given the country's location high in the Andes Mountains, the War of the Pacific left Bolivia landlocked.

Debates between conservatives and liberals were also not unique to Mexico. While few countries devolved into civil conflict, the period from 1850 to 1870 witnessed a wide implementation of **liberal reforms**. These included a number *of judicial, social, and land-holding reforms, but economically, the liberal reforms refer to "the social and political process involved in workers gaining their freedom and becoming mobile and in turning land into a tradable asset."*[17] Thus, the same 1857 Constitution that minimized the Catholic Church and sparked the Wars of Reform was also key in making loans easier to obtain. Prior to 1857, entrepreneurs looking for loans were limited by the interest rates that lenders could charge. The Catholic Church's strong influence in Latin America manifested in limits on interest rates, known as anti-usuary laws. In Mexico, interest rates on loans could not be higher than 6 percent, but in such a volatile and untested space, new ventures were often riskier, and investors saw the risks as too costly, making for minimal investments. In other words, only the elite could pursue untested ventures that had the potential for high pay-offs and rewards.

Ironically, Maximilian, the ill-fated European monarch in Mexico, upheld many of the liberal reforms enacted by the 1861 Constitution, meaning structural changes occurred that would lead toward bank development, opening new domestic opportunities for loans. It was during Maximilian's tenure that Mexico's textile industry resurged, and the Mexico-Veracruz Railroad began to be constructed. Thus, despite the incredible chaos, elite and middle-class entrepreneurs were finally able to secure loans to finance new businesses, expand current ventures, or invest in new technology. Similar banking revolutions occurred in Chile, Brazil, Argentina, and Peru. In Brazil, the 1850 Commercial Code privatized the banks, but the fact that it was government officials who controlled banks and then privatized those banks in order to gain finance for themselves stunted credit market growth. The **joint-stock company** that *allowed groups of individuals to pool resources and credit to incorporate and start new ventures* required large loans and considerable investments, meaning credit was still restricted to the traditional landed classes, socially connected politicians, or burgeoning industrialists. Access to smaller loans for the general population was still well over half a century away.

Notes

1 This excludes mainland colonies of Great Britain (Belize and Guyana), the Netherlands (Suriname), and France (French Guiana).
2 Between 1814 and 1825, six negotiations took place between Haiti and its former colonizer.
3 Mandiou, "The Separation of Haiti and the Dominican Republic," p. 97.
4 Price observations from Seward, *Reminiscences of a Wartime Diplomat*, pp. 318–19. Seward noted one day's supply for the ship amounted to 100 Haitian gourdes, the equivalent of 6 gold US dollars.
5 The fact that taxes on trade funded most of Chile and Brazil's deficits was a measure of a relative peaceful nineteenth century in those nations, not export growth.
6 Seward, *Reminiscences of a Wartime Diplomat*, p. 317.
7 Chile also experienced a degree of stability.
8 Oscar Zanetti Lecuona and Alejando García Alvarez, *Sugar & Railroads*, p. 17.
9 Sugar beet production expanded during the Napoleonic Wars (1799–1815) when supplies of imported sugar were cut off. After the wars, national governments began subsidizing sugar beet production.
10 Henochsberg, "Public Debt and Slavery," pp. 31, 35.
11 Aguilar Avilés and Lindo-Fuentes, *Un vistazo al pasado de la educación en El Salvador*.
12 In Mexico, for example, the Church remained strong, meaning that the Church and state often operated alongside one another.
13 Morrisson and Murtin, "The Century of Education."
14 Most of the combatants were either from French colonies or they were Mexican mestizos.
15 See references in Vaughan and Lewis, eds. *Eagle and the Virgin* for the importance of the Virgin Mary.
16 Whigham, *The Paraguayan War*, says 70 percent of the population of 450,000 died, p. xiv.
17 Bértola and Ocampo, *Economic History*, p. 70.

Suggested Media, Literature, and Digital Resources

Altamirano, Ignacio Manuel, Ronald J. Christ, and Sheridan Phillips. *El Zarco, the Blue-Eyed Bandit: Episodes of Mexican Life between 1861–1863*. Santa Fe: Lumen Books, 2007.

"Banco de la República Virtual Library." Banco de la República. Accessed January 22, 2024. https://babel.banrepcultural.org/digital/collection/p17054coll26.

Callcott, Lady Maria. *Journal of a Voyage to Brazil: and Residence There During Part of the Years 1821, 1822, 1823*. London, n.d.

National Library of Brasil. "Brasil's Hemeroteca Nacional." Accessed January 22, 2024. https://bndigital.bn.gov.br/hemeroteca-digital/.

Porter, Catherine, Constant Méheut, Matt Apuzzo, and Selam Gebrekidan. "Haiti 'Ransom' Project." *New York Times*. November 16, 2022. https://www.nytimes.com/spotlight/haiti.

Sarmiento, Domingo Faustino. *Facundo: civilización y barbarie en la República Argentina*. Spain: Editorial-América, 1916.

Seward, Frederick W. *Reminiscences of a War-Time Statesman and Diplomat 1830–1915*. New York: G.P. Putnam's Sons, The Knickerbocker Press, 1916.

Select Bibliography

Aguilar Avilés, Gilberto and Héctor Lindo-Fuentes. *Un vistazo al pasado de la educación en El Salvador*. San Salvador: Ministerio de Educación, 1995.

Bates, Robert H., John H. Coatsworth, and Jeffrey G. Williamson. "Lost Decades: Post Independence Performance in Latin America and Africa." *The Journal of Economic History* 67, no. 4 (2007): 917–43.

Benavot, Aaron, and Phyllis Riddle. "The Expansion of Primary Education, 1870–1940: Trends and Issues." *Sociology of Education* 61, no. 3 (1988): 191–210.

Bértola, Luis, and José Antonio Ocampo. *The Economic Development of Latin America since Independence*. Oxford: Oxford University Press, 2012.

Bleynat, Ingrid. *Vendors' Capitalism: A Political Economy of Public Markets in Mexico City*. Stanford: Stanford University Press, 2021.

Bonilla, Heraclio. "Peru and Bolivia from Independence to the War of the Pacific." *The Cambridge History of Latin America* 3 (1985): 539–82.

Cázarez Mata, José Trinidad. "Formando ciudadanos." *Relatos e Historia en México* 125, (January 2019). https://relatosehistorias.mx/la-coleccion/125-violencia-y-terror-en-la-independencia-de-mexico.

Daut, Marlene. *Tropics of Haiti: Race and the Literary History of the Haitian Revolution in the Atlantic World, 1789–1865*. Liverpool: Liverpool University Press, 2015.

Dubois, Laurent, Kaiama L. Glover, Nadève Ménard, Millery Polyné, and Cahntalle F. Verna, eds. *The Haiti Reader: History Culture, Politics*. Durham: Duke University Press, 2020. https://muse.jhu.edu/book/72252.

Eichengreen, Barry, and Peter H. Lindert, Eds. *The International Debt Crisis in Historical Perspective*. Cambridge: Massachusetts Institute of Technology Press, 1989.

Fick, Carolyn. "Revolutionary St. Domingue and the Emerging Atlantic: Paradigms of Sovereignty." In *The Haitian Revolution and the Early United States: Histories, Textualities, Geographies*, edited by Elizabeth Maddock Dillon and Michael Drexler, 141–66. Philadelphia: University of Pennsylvania Press, 2016.

Flandreau, Marc, and Juan H. Flores. "Bonds and Brands: Foundations of Sovereign Debt Markets, 1820–1830." *The Journal of Economic History* 69, no. 3 (2009): 646–84.

Halperin, Ernst. *The National Liberation Movements in Latin America*. Project on Communism, Revisionism, and Revolution, Center for International Studies, Massachusetts Institute of Technology, 1969.

Hanley, Anne G. *The Public Good and the Brazilian State: Municipal Finance and Public Services in São Paulo, 1822–1930*. Chicago: University of Chicago Press, 2018. https://doi.org/10.7208/9780226535104.

Henochsberg, Simon. "Public Debt and Slavery: The Case of Haiti (1760–1915)." Paris School of Economics, December 2016. http://www.piketty.pse.ens.fr/files/Henochsberg2016.pdf.

Irigoin, Alejandra. "The End of a Silver Era: The Consequences of the Breakdown of the Spanish Peso Standard in China and the United States, 1780s–1850s." *Journal of World History* 20, no. 2 (2009): 207–44.

Kalmanovitz, Salomón. *Nueva Historia Económica de Colombia*. Bogotá: Taurus and Universidade Jorge Tadeo Lozano, 2010.

Levy, Juliette. "Una Cuestión De Intereses: Entre Benito, Maximiliano y Porfirio. Una Reforma Liberal y La Liberación De Tasas De Interés En Yucatán, 1850–1900." *America Latina En La Historia Económica* 19, no. 1 (2012): 157–77.

Lorenzo, Tania Garcia, and Milagros Martinez Reinosa. "Six Lessons from Haiti: The Need for Cooperation and Development." *The International Journal of Cuban Studies* 2, no. 3/4 (2010): 301–14.

Mandiou, Thomas. "The Separation of Haiti and the Dominican Republic." In *The Haiti Reader: History Culture, Politics*, edited by Laurent Dubois, Kaiama L. Glover, Nadève Ménard, Millery Polyné, and Cahntalle F. Verna, 97–99. Durham: Duke University Press, 2020.

Marichal, Carlos. *A Century of Debt Crisis in Latin America: From Independence to the Great Depression, 1820–1930*. Princeton: Princeton University Press, 1989.

Martin Acena, Pablo, and Jaime Reis, eds. *Monetary Standards in the Periphery: Paper, Silver and Gold, 1854–1933*. New York: St. Martin's Press, 2000.

Méndez Pereira, Octavio. *Historia de la Instrucción Pública en Panamá*. Panama: Biblioteca de la Nacionalidad, Autoridad del Canal de Panamá, 1999, 249–320. http://bdigital.binal.ac.pa/bdp/tomoXIIP2.pdf.

Morrisson, Christian, and Fabrice Murtin. "The Century of Education." *Journal of Human Capital* 3, no. 1 (2009): 1–42. https://doi.org/10.1086/600102.

Obregón, Liliana. "Empire, Racial Capitalism and International Law: The Case of Manumitted Haiti and the Recognition Debt." *Leiden Journal of International Law* 31, no. 3 (2018): 597–615.

Phillips, Anthony. "Haiti, France and the Independence Debt of 1825." *Canada Haiti Action Network* 24 (2008): 1–24.

Pita Rico, Roger. "Los colegios en Colombia en los primeros años de vida republicana, 1819–1828." *Educación y Ciencia* 18: 137–58.

Popkin, Jeremy D. "Consolidating Independence in a Hostile World." In *Haiti: An Introduction*, 141–66. Oxford: Wiley-Blackwell, 2011.

Stein, Robert L. "From Saint Domingue to Haiti, 1804–1825." *The Journal of Caribbean History* 19, no. 2 (1984): 189–226.

Summerhill, William R. *Inglorious Revolution: Political Institutions, Sovereign Debt, and Financial Underdevelopment in Imperial Brazil*. New Haven: Yale University Press, 2015.

Taylor, Alan M., and Jeffrey G. Williamson. "Capital Flows to the New World as an Intergenerational Transfer." *The Journal of Political Economy* 102, no. 2 (1994): 348–71. https://doi.org/10.1086/261935.
Vaughan, Mary Kay. "Primary Education and Literacy in Nineteenth-Century Mexico: Research Trends, 1968–1988." *Latin American Research Review* 25, no. 1 (1990): 31–66. http://www.jstor.org/stable/2503559.
Vaughan, Mary Kay, and Stephen Lewis, eds. *The Eagle and the Virgin: Nation and Cultural Revolution in Mexico, 1920–1940*. Durham: Duke University Press, 2006.
Vizcarra, Catalina. "Guano, Credible Commitments, and Sovereign Debt Repayment in Nineteenth-Century Peru." *The Journal of Economic History* 69, no. 2 (2009): 358–87.
Whigham, Thomas L. *The Paraguayan War: Causes and Early Conduct*. Calgary: University of Calgary Press, 2018.
Zanetti Lecuona, Oscar, and Alejandro García Alvarez. *Sugar & Railroads: A Cuban History, 1837–1959*. Translated by Franklin W. Knight and Mary Todd. Chapel Hill: University of North Carolina Press, 1998.

3 Export-led Growth (1870–1930): Part I

Between 1870 and 1930, relative political stability and technological advancements ushered in a new phase in Latin America's economic history: export-oriented growth. A land-abundant region with rich mineral wealth and agricultural potential, Latin America could export raw materials, foodstuffs (cacao, wheat, coffee), and mining commodities (copper, silver, nitrates) that industrialized nations and their populations demanded. Latin America's exports per capita more than doubled between 1870 and 1912, and the region's share of world exports accounted for nearly 8 percent by 1930. Countries tended to specialize in one to three exports, making them highly susceptible to changes in market prices. In Brazil, where coffee comprised over 60 percent of all exports, the government enacted extreme measures – buying and even burning excess coffee to artificially control global coffee prices when bumper crops or declining prices threatened revenues.

During the same period, immigration and some improvements in life expectancy meant growing populations. The growing demands of both the export and domestic markets led to considerable changes in how land, labor, capital, and entrepreneurship were used. These inputs, when considered collectively, are known as factors of production.[1] In Latin America during this period, expanding production often relied on changes to the labor, land, and capital parts of the equation that further marginalized some populations and often saw export interests trump domestic demands. When data are available, for example, it shows that while export production per capita increased, overall production per capita largely decreased. After World War I, Argentina, Uruguay, and Mexico saw improvements in GDP per capita, but that metric continued to decline in Brazil and Cuba.

The next two chapters explore the interplay of factors of production during Latin America's period of export-led growth. Reflecting an important change to labor was Brazil's **1871 Rio Branco law**. This free womb law marked an important step toward complete abolition in 1888. Independence had set off a process of gradual abolition in much of Latin

DOI: 10.4324/9781003283843-3

America, but Brazil and Cuba continued to import enslaved Africans through the middle of the nineteenth century, primarily to work on coffee and sugar plantations, respectively. Like other countries that had already abolished slavery, both simultaneously explored alternate labor regimes. A combination of migrant and immigrant flows (within and to the region) ensured an abundance of low-wage labor for both the export and domestic markets. These flows facilitated a trend of general labor exploitation, while discrimination created differentiated labor experiences.

Accompanying this labor transition were important capital changes facilitating larger-scale projects. As trains and steamships reduced transportation costs, and liberal reforms allowed for reduced risk, investors, particularly foreign investors, took note and Latin American capital markets grew. The **1891 Baring Crisis** demonstrates the scale of that investment, the global interconnectedness that larger countries in the region achieved in a relatively short amount of time, and the region's susceptibility to volatility.

Both transitions highlight the role that Europeans and Europe played in the region's export-led growth period, particularly in the Southern Cone. The connection included the millions of Italian, Spanish, and Portuguese immigrant workers flowing to the ports of Buenos Aires, Montevideo, Rio de Janeiro, Maracaibo, and Havana. It involved the imported consumer products, machinery, and foodstuffs that the domestic market could not supply, and it encompassed the British and European capitalists investing in railways and other industrial ventures. The Atlantic tie was strong, only fully disrupted by World War I, which significantly slowed the flow of people, imports, and capital alike.

Rio Branco Law, 1871 (Rio de Janeiro, Brazil)

On September 28, 1871, Brazil's Congress passed the Rio Branco Law declaring that any child born in Brazil after the date was free, as long as they gave their services to their mother's masters from ages 8 to 21 years. This was the last free womb law passed in the region and a critical step toward full abolition of slavery. On May 13, 1888, Brazil would be the last country to abolish slavery in Latin America. The Rio Branco Law demonstrates not only the challenges that slavery and continued discrimination brought to the region's development, but also highlights the transition to wage-based labor in the region that gained traction toward the end of the nineteenth century.

Ten years after the law was passed, an enslaved woman living in Rio de Janeiro, Cândida, gave birth to a daughter, Georgina. Georgina was technically born free, but this did not stop her mother's master from auctioning off her services in Rio's *Jornal do Comercio* to the highest bidder in 1882. In the same year, one-year-old Adele Bertoldi arrived in São Paulo from

Italy along with her family of five.[2] They had left Genoa and were on their way to Campinas, likely to find work on the coffee plantations. Although these two young girls never met, their lives and their families' lives, and those of thousands like them, were inextricably shaped by slavery.

Outside of Haiti, abolition did not come with a revolt. In most countries it was a gradual process that included de jure and de facto abolition of the transatlantic slave trade, free womb laws, and finally decrees of abolition. Abolitionists, liberals, and enslaved people alike made significant contributions toward the process, with enslaved participation in military campaigns playing particular importance. For those countries not heavily reliant on slavery in the late colonial period, independence was an important step toward abolition. Mexico, Chile, and Central America abolished slavery at or shortly after independence. Independence also factored into gradual abolition in Uruguay, Ecuador, Colombia, Argentina, Peru, and Venezuela. During the Independence Wars, royalists often extended the promise of emancipation if the enslaved would join their ranks. As the wars waged on, leaders like Simón Bolívar came to understand that abolition would be key to successful liberation from Spain, passing free womb laws with independence. The timing meant abolition was achieved in the middle of the nineteenth century in much of the region during the era of liberalism. Slavery persisted about a decade longer in Bolivia and Paraguay, but the size of the enslaved population was small in each of these countries.

At the time of the Independence Wars, slavery was much more prominent in the Caribbean and Brazil. In the case of the Dominican Republic, abolition came when Haiti occupied Santo Domingo, bringing freedom for those living on the eastern side of Hispaniola. For Puerto Rico, Cuba, and Brazil, the institution persisted into the export-led growth period. Puerto Rico and Cuba remained colonies of Spain until 1899. Until 1889, Brazil was its own empire with a constitutional monarchy. Outside of Haiti, the three were also the blackest. Roughly half of Cuba's and Puerto Rico's populations and about 60 percent of Brazil's population were Black or Afro-descended. As other nations took steps toward abolition, Cuba and Brazil saw an increased dependence on slavery in the first half of the nineteenth century. This growth occurred despite technical abolition of the transatlantic slave trade in 1820. The share of disembarkations *increased* to both countries in the 1830s. Known slaving voyages continued to occur through 1850 in Brazil and 1866 in Cuba. It was not until the effective end of the transatlantic slave trade that steps toward abolition gained popularity in Cuba and Brazil.

Both areas had benefited from relative stability in the nineteenth century and had thriving export agricultural sectors that required substantial labor forces. Cuba filled much of the sugar industry void that Haiti left after the Haitian Revolution, becoming the world's largest sugar producer in the 1850s. Over 800,000 enslaved Africans would be brought onto the island, making 43 percent of the population enslaved. In Brazil, coffee production expanded substantially, becoming Brazil's chief export by 1833. Over 2.4 million enslaved Africans would come to Brazil in the nineteenth century. While the number was substantial, Brazil's dependence on slavery at this moment concentrated in the southeast and even there, provincial differences saw diminished dependence on slavery once the slave trade was effectively abolished. In 1825, one-third of Brazil's Afro-descended population was enslaved; in 1850 the share was 25 percent and one year after Brazil passed its free womb law, the share had diminished further to 15 percent.

As in the case of abolition elsewhere in the region, military service factored into abolition in both countries. In Brazil, many owners offered enslaved workers freedom to take their place in the unpopular Paraguay War (1864–1870). When these veterans returned triumphant, and now free, many moved to urban centers and pressured for general abolition. In the case of Cuba, rebels offered emancipation to men who would join their fight against Spain for independence in the Ten Years' War (1868–1878).[3] Spain provided a counteroffer of eventual abolition, passing the Moret Law (free womb) in Cuba and Puerto Rico in 1870, just one year before Brazil's Rio Branco Law.

Abolition created a new potential workforce in these countries, but prejudice, discrimination, and low **human capital** – *training, education, health, and experience accumulated over a lifetime* – could prevent the full integration of many of the former enslaved. For Brazil's Southeast, scholars have also found occupational discrimination increased for Blacks after abolition. While excluded from liberal professional and healthcare jobs, Blacks were overrepresented in domestic service. At first Black Cubans seemed to fare a bit better in terms of education. In 1861, 38.5 percent of whites above the age of 7 were literate, while the rate for Blacks was a mere 5.3 percent. By 1907, almost 70 percent of Cuba's white 10–19-year-olds were literate, and the rate for non-white Cubans just a bit behind at 67 percent. Gains were substantial for boys and girls, white and non-white, but this achievement did not necessarily translate into higher education or equal job opportunities. At the university level, despite being more than 25 percent of Cuba's population, the only degree where non-whites represented more than 15 percent of the student population was in dentistry: in law, medicine, engineering, and even in agricultural expertise, whites achieved 89–98 percent of degrees. The gap widened after 1907, and by 1931 white Cubans were 4 percentage points higher than non-whites in terms of obtaining university titles.

The inability to fully include emancipated slaves and their descendants is further complicated by the multiple immigration projects that defined the era. Even before abolition, increased labor needs from an expanding export market motivated plantation owners to explore alternate labor forces. In Brazil, railroads expanded the coffee frontier into São Paulo and Minas Gerais. The expansion created considerable labor demand to both build the railways and work the coffee harvest. In Cuba, railroads along with improved sugar mill technology allowed for sugar cane cultivation on the island's eastern frontiers. Chinese "coolies," unskilled laborers often forced into slave-like debt peonage, and unskilled Spanish immigrants, many of whom were indentured servants, arrived on the island.[4] They built railroads and worked on sugar plantations. In Miguel Barnet's *Biography of a Runaway Slave*, Esteban Montejo recounts his life on Cuban plantations. Not only are Lucumí, Carabalí, and Congo practices detailed, but so too is the presence of Chinese coolies. In all, over 700,000 Chinese would come to Latin America, their presence becoming most significant in Cuba and Peru.

In addition to Chinese arrivals, colonization strategies were discussed and established in most Latin American countries. Governments in Chile, Brazil, and even Paraguay and Mexico, countries with considerable mestizo and Indigenous populations, established immigrant settler colonies beginning in the 1830s. Liberal politicians lauded immigration as a part of their transition toward more modern agriculture. German colonies found success in Chile and southern Brazil. Chile suspended its restriction of non-Catholic immigrants to encourage settlement in its southern regions. Welsh colonies in Patagonia and French colonies in Argentina were also successful. As abolition progressed, former investors in the slave trade and slave owners looked for alternate ways to invest their money, including immigration and transportation companies. It is unsurprising, then, that starting in 1840, European arrivals surpassed African arrivals in Latin America.

In Brazil, while Chinese coolies were introduced and some settler colonies found success, it was the European immigrant settler families arriving after 1871 who began the true transition away from enslaved labor. In the same year that Brazil passed its free womb law, São Paulo coffee planters established the Society to Aid Immigration. The society was to subsidize European *colono* agricultural families to work on coffee plantations. These settler communities brought groups of a similar background together to develop the coffee economy. If families agreed to sign a contract to work on the plantation for a year, the society would pay for transatlantic passage, cover food costs, and connect the family to coffee plantation owners. Recruiting European families would encourage permanency, keep a large supply of unskilled labor (keeping labor costs low), and would work toward an official policy of "whitening" that valorized whiteness at the expense of Afro- and Indigenous-descended populations. While not consciously aware of these currents, the young Adele Bertoldi and her family were part of this movement.

Families accepting the Brazilian subsidies were often Europeans of the least means, for whom paid passage was the only viable option for migration across the Atlantic. Those in better circumstances often opted to finance the voyage themselves or through social networks. Most headed to Argentina, Brazil, and Uruguay, although Cuba became a more popular destination after 1900. The global depression of 1873, demographic pressures in Europe, the agricultural revolution, and industrialization pushed them out of Europe. Latin America, now more stable, pulled them toward jobs as foreign and domestic entrepreneurs invested in railroad and export-oriented production. Urbanization and more diverse industrialization for domestic markets followed, making Latin America's Southern Cone an important node in the **international labor market** *where workers considered relative wages in their calculations to migrate*. Improved steamships made Atlantic passages cheaper, making seasonal migration a common phenomenon, particularly among Italian immigrants (particularly in Argentina). As many as 50 percent of arriving Italian migrants returned, but this also meant that 50 percent stayed.

Population growth was one of the main drivers of production growth during the period. Latin America's population grew by 1.5 percent during the period of export-oriented growth, but the rate was almost double that figure in Argentina, Uruguay, and Southeast Brazil, the centers of European immigration. For Argentina and Uruguay, these movements meant the Euro-descended population came to dominate the wage labor market. Wheat, linen, and corn production in these temperate climates had a comparative advantage and Latin America's new frontier offered higher relative wages than Europe. Products grown in tropical climates, however, were often in competition with those grown in Africa and Asia, regions that could produce similar products more cheaply due to lower labor costs.

Immigrants used social networks and immigrant recruitment companies to learn where they could earn the highest real wages, but they also considered factors such as language and cultural compatibility. Northern Italians with industrial skills could count on stiff competition and discrimination in the United States, but they found ready work in railroad companies or in rapidly industrializing Southern Cone cities like Buenos Aires and São Paulo. An immigrant's own words in a letter to his parents in 1910 best details the importance that family, hometown, and language proximity played in the labor market:

> I am no longer in Buenos Aires since I have taken on a project for the construction of a railroad to go from Santa Fe to Dean Funes ... Right Now I have fifty-seven workmen, but in a little while there will be many more. There are also some Biellesi[5] with me, all masons, who came

> especially for this ... For this project ... I have as my chief assistant and friend an old school friend Mr. Secondo Cravello.[6]

Europeans and Chinese were not the only arrivals to the region. Notable Japanese and Lebanese migrations also occurred. Starting in 1908, as the United States closed its doors to Japanese immigrants through the Gentleman's Agreement, a bilateral agreement between Japan and Brazil brought Okinawans to work on coffee plantations. Japan also negotiated with Argentina, Chile, Ecuador, Mexico, and Peru, but Brazil became the dominant receiver of Japanese migration to the Americas. Here, the *colono* model, rather than male contract laborers, became the dominant migration form. Over the course of the twentieth century, over 200,000 Japanese would arrive in Brazil, with São Paulo today housing the largest population of Japanese outside of Japan.

Like Lebanese and Chinese arrivals to Brazil and to the region, Japanese occupied an ambiguous racial categorization. They were not white, Black, or Indigenous, an identity that they retained through high endogamy rates. Hyphenated identities did not protect them from discrimination, but often proved advantageous in the agricultural and business realms. Japanese disproportionately owned cotton and rice farms in Peru and Brazil, respectively, and Lebanese came to find considerable commercial success in dry goods, and then textiles. Commercial success paved the way for political opportunities. One hundred years later, leaders like Mexico's business magnate Carlos Slim or ex-presidents such as Alberto Fujimori in Peru and Carlos Menem in Argentina, trace their roots to these migrations. Influence of non-European immigration is palpable in every realm, from neighborhoods like São Paulo's Liberdade and Havana's Barrio Chino to food traditions like Mexico's *tacos árabes*, and even in the rhythms of early music released by Colombia's iconic artist Shakira (Isabel Mebarak Ripoll).

Immigration's greatest relative impact was in Argentina, where over 3.8 million immigrants settled between 1881 and 1930, although the influx to Brazil's Southeast region was also substantial. Between 1860 and 1900, Argentina had the highest immigration rate in all the Americas (including the United States). By the start of World War I, almost one-third of Argentina's population and eight out of ten adult males were foreign-born. Immigrants came to work on the expanding agricultural frontier or as laborers in the burgeoning industrial sector. Most eventually found jobs in cities, in companies owned by their more affluent compatriots; when employment was unpredictable, they moved or made their own opportunities.

Even in countries with smaller immigration rates, the economic impact could be disproportionately large. While just 7 percent of Chile's population was foreign-born in 1907, by 1914, foreigners owned 32 and 49 percent of commercial and industrial firms, respectively. It was in these establishments and in neighborhoods where immigrant nationals often bonded, establishing a variety of formal institutions from mutual aid societies and schools to foreign-language newspapers and soccer clubs. While soccer first arrived in the continent through British railway companies, it was in neighborhood and factory clubs that it took on national significance. Many of today's prominent soccer clubs, like Brazil's Vasco da Gama and Palmeiras, Chile's Club Palestino, and Argentina's San Lorenzo, trace their roots to ethnic clubs. Even in Mexico, which never experienced wide-scale immigration, miners from Cornwall, England working in Pachuca's mine owned by William Blamey, a British national, were at the heart of establishing the Pachuca Athletic Club in 1901. The club's legacy continues today as Pachuca F.C., consistently competing in Mexico's top soccer division.

Baring Crisis, 1891 (London, England)

When Europe began to emerge from the Depression of 1873, immigrants were not the only ones who found Latin America attractive: the resource-rich region drew European and American investors, too. To invest required solving a financial conundrum. Most Latin American countries had achieved relative political stability, but many national governments continued to default on loan payments.[7] Investment, thus, skyrocketed in private initiatives, particularly in Argentina, Mexico, Brazil, Chile, and Uruguay. About one-third of the region's **capital stock**, *the shares issued to finance initiatives and growth*, was foreign. Railroads accounted for over 60 percent of London investments in the region. Investors also funded public utilities, industrial ventures, and urban renewal campaigns. The latter added a Parisian and European flair to colonial street patterns as streets widened, water supplies and public lighting improved, and public parks and municipal opera houses opened. Attracting more investment required attractive cities and modern comforts. These initiatives were further justified by emerging pseudo-scientific ideas that more modern and "civilized" structures could elevate the local populations, the majority of whom had a mixture of European, African, and Indigenous backgrounds.

As early as the 1860s some foreigners were attracted to investment that could be characterized as investing in infrastructure (like railroads) to grow export economies (wheat, hides, cotton, sugar, etc.). The rationale was that revenues would increase from those exports and countries would be able to pay back the loans with interest. During this decade, Argentina represented 30 percent of foreign loans. By the 1870s, export-generated revenues lagged and, hoping to continue to expand, Argentine leaders raised export production and increasingly turned to state banks rather than foreign lenders. Then an Argentine banking reform allowed banks to print more paper currency, providing people with more access to credit. Subsequently, banks printed 18 percent more of the new paper currency to satisfy a growing demand. Inflation followed and the Argentine peso was devalued in comparison to other world currencies. By the end of the 1880s, it was apparent that Argentina would not be able to make its debt payments to London investors, which had been issued in currencies backed with sterling or gold, not the devalued Argentine peso. In 1890, Argentina entered a recession and defaulted on a nearly £48-million debt.

On the other side of the Atlantic, Argentina's default led to investor panic. Argentina accounted for 40 to 50 percent of all British lending outside of the United Kingdom. The default brought the British Baring Bank to the brink of failure. The Bank of England and the Rothschilds, who had backed many of the loans, realized Baring Brothers was "too big to fail" and triggered what Mitchener and Weidenmeier have termed a "rescue operation" to save the bank. Drawing on resources from English financial institutions, as well as Russian and French central banks, England's central bank pooled resources to create a rescue fund, pulling the House of Baring from the brink of bankruptcy. That rescue, however, did not extend to Argentina and the Baring Crisis tarnished the region's reputation. From Chile, Colombia, Honduras, Nicaragua, and Brazil, prompt in making debt payments, European lenders reduced investments in the region.[8]

At the time of the Baring Crisis, Argentina, like most of Latin America, was not on the gold standard. This meant that monetary transactions occurred using a combination of paper currency, coins, and notes that could be converted into either gold or silver at a specific bank. Foreign debt payments needed to be paid in gold, but other tender was the norm for daily transactions and national banks. This meant that currencies were particularly susceptible to changes in the global value of these metals. When silver faced global **devaluation**, or *a reduction in its value relative to other currencies* in the 1880s, currencies lost value. Printing more paper money did not resolve the problem; it just produced a conflict between monetary policy (printing money and interest rates) and fiscal policy (taxes and spending).

The Baring Crisis was far from the only banking failure and fiscal crisis in the region, illustrating that despite making headway during the export-led-growth period, capital markets related to long-term investments, and banking and financial institutions, remained underdeveloped in the region. In the Brazilian *Encilhamento*, for example, an 1890 law allowed firms to invest beyond the value of the money they had in reserves. The resulting boom saw over 200 new companies and banks formed in just six months (where before there had been just 30). Just as quickly, the speculative frenzy saw bankruptcies and failures. By the end of the nineteenth century, with increasing inflation, Brazil was in dire need of another banking reform.

In Mexico, stable banks and reliable credit markets had been slower to develop. The development and protection of joint-stock companies, which allowed for pooling resources to invest in a venture, spurred investments and the banking sector began to grow. As confidence grew, lending interest rates to the government dropped and investment in government ventures increased. A fiscal crisis in 1895 was even weathered by Banamex, whose reputation saw it develop regional branches and multiple agents by 1900. Investment rates evened out across regions and between public and private investments, leading to greater capital market integration. While a more stable economic environment meant Mexico did not suffer a speculative crisis like Brazil, it came with a tradeoff: it restricted markets and credit largely to the elite. Smaller loans to start up small businesses or to buy homes or merchandise were effectively impossible. Ultimately, this meant that wealth gained through investments continued to accumulate in the hands of a few.

Despite the fiscal crises between 1870 and 1913, Europe remained attuned to the Latin American market. On the eve of the World War I, British investors still had over £1.2 billion ($5.8 billion) invested in the region, the French $1.7 billion, the United States $1.6 billion, and Germans $678 million. The war once again challenged currencies' stability. European conflict cut off new loans and imports of most finished products and machinery. In 1913, over 75 percent of Latin American imports came from the United Kingdom, Germany, France, and the United States. The resulting drop cut off imports and customs revenues, raising prices exorbitantly in Latin America. Some countries, such as Chile, fared better because the demand of their chief exports increased during the war, but a push both internationally and within Latin America for currency stability brought about a move toward **fixed exchange rates** in the post-war era. *National currencies would be exchanged with another national currency in a set ratio, but that currency did need to be fully convertible into gold.* It was in this context that the United States dollar became the currency exchange of choice for Latin America. Central banks were an accompanying reform, eliminating the days when a bank could issue its own currency. Reforms, however, did not bring about the hoped-for stability. By 1926, much of Latin America was already experiencing the start of the Great Depression.

The vast majority of Latin America's population could not access these expanded credit markets, did not invest in factory-sized ventures, and played no role in discussions surrounding exchange rates. These changes still impacted them significantly. When countries had to spend more of the national budget servicing debt because of devalued currencies, this left less to provide social services for the general population. Reduced investment or a lack of machinery imports could bring about reduced work hours. For the typical day laborer, or unskilled or service worker, the unpredictable currency changes and fluctuations made planning increasingly difficult and living more expensive.[9] Whereas one or two incomes may have been able to support a household in the 1880s and '90s, households became increasingly dependent on several incomes just to make ends meet. If a family or individual was unable to meet their expenses, they had to turn to their credit network, borrowing from family and friends, calling on mutual aid societies, or resorting to informal employment, pawning clothes, tools, and furniture. Urban environments leant themselves to these support networks, but outside of the Southern Cone and Cuba, most Latin Americans lived in rural settings. The agriculture sector and rural life dominated the daily experiences of the region's population.

Notes

1 The output made from the combined factors of production are known as the production function. The Cobb-Douglas production function considers just land and capital as the factors of production.
2 On Georgina, see Conrad, *Children of God's Fire*, p. 341. For Adele, see "Registros de Matrícula" Hospedaria de Immigrantes de São Paulo, book 1, pp. 42–43, https://acervodigital.museudaimigracao.org.br/upload/livros/pdfs/L001_043.pdf. Unfortunately, we have no further records to be able to track these two girls' lives.
3 The offer of freedom was not extended to women or non-veterans.
4 The term "coolie" is used here to reflect the slave-like conditions that laborers endured. It is important to note, however, that although "coolie" was originally a British bureaucratic term for indentured laborers, it "became a highly charged slur." National Public Radio, November 19, 2013. "'Coolie Woman' Rescues Indentured Women from Anonymity." Transcript of *Tell Me More*. https://www.npr.org/2013/11/19/246154506/coolie-woman-rescues-indentured-women-from-anonymity.
5 Biellesi refers to Italians from the northern piedmont.
6 Baily and Ramella, *One Family, Two Worlds*, p. 97.
7 Most countries experienced stability during this period; however, there were some notable exceptions. The War of the Pacific between Chile, Bolivia, and Peru (1870–1876); Colombia's War of a Thousand Days, the Spanish-American War in Cuba and Puerto Rico, and the Mexican Revolution.
8 For another discussion of contagion, see the 1982 Peso Crisis and the 1998 Asian market crisis (Chapter 6).
9 Theoretically, production in Latin America should have been cheaper with devalued currencies. In this scenario, production would increase, providing more jobs and releasing labor market pressure. Competing export and industrial sectors and labor exploitation often hindered this growth.

Suggested Media, Literature, and Digital Resources

Azevedo, Aluísio, and David H. Rosenthal. *The Slum: A Novel*. Oxford: Oxford University Press, 2000.
"The Baring Archive Digitised Collections." ING. Accessed November 1, 2023. https://baring.access.preservica.com.
Eltis, David. "A Brief Overview of the Trans-Atlantic Slave Trade." *Slave Voyages: The Trans-Atlantic Slave Trade Database*. Accessed April 27, 2018. https://www.slavevoyages.org/voyage/about.
Montejo, Esteban, Miguel Barnet, and W. Nick Hill. *Biography of a Runaway Slave*, revised edition. Willimantic: Curbstone Press, 1994.

Select Bibliography

Alonso, Blanca Sánchez. "The Other Europeans: Immigration into Latin America and the International Labour Market (1870–1930)." *Revista de Historia Económica* 25, no. 3 (2007): 395–426. https://doi.org/10.1017/S0212610900000185.
Andrews, George Reid. *Afro-Latin America, 1800–2000*. Oxford: Oxford University Press, 2004.
Baily, Samuel L., and Franco Ramella, eds. *One Family, Two Worlds: An Italian Family's Correspondence across the Atlantic, 1901–1922*. Translated by John Lenaghan. New Brunswick: Rutgers University Press, 1988.
Baily, Samuel L. *Immigrants in the Lands of Promise: Italians in Buenos Aires and New York City, 1870–1914*. Ithaca: Cornell University Press, 2003.
Ball, Molly C. *Navigating Life and Work in Old Republic São Paulo*. Gainesville: University of Florida Press, 2020.
Bucciferro, Justin R. "Racial Inequality in Brazil from Independence to the Present." In *Has Latin American Inequality Changed Direction? Looking Over the Long Run*, 2017, 171–94.
Cahill, Kevin J. "The US Bank Panic of 1907 and the Mexican Depression of 1908–1909." *The Historian* 60, no. 4 (1998): 795–811.
Cárdenas, Enrique, José Antonio Ocampo, and Rosemary Thorp, eds. *An Economic History of Twentieth-Century Latin America. Volume 1. The Export Age: The Latin American Economies in the Late Nineteenth and Early Twentieth Centuries*. New York: Palgrave, 2000.
Chazkel, Amy. *Laws of Chance: Brazil's Clandestine Lottery and the Making of Urban Public Life*. Duke University Press, 2011.
Coatsworth, John H. "Indispensable Railroads in a Backward Economy: The Case of Mexico." *The Journal of Economic History* 39, no. 4 (1979): 939–60.
Conde, Roberto Cortes. "Export-Led Growth in Latin America: 1870–1930." *Journal of Latin American Studies* 24, no. S1 (1992): 163–79.
Conrad, Robert Edgar. *Children of God's Fire: A Documentary History of Black Slavery in Brazil*. University Park: Pennsylvania State University Press, 1994.
Cowling, Camillia. "Negotiating Freedom: Women of Colour and the Transition to Free Labour in Cuba, 1870–1886." *Slavery & Abolition* 26, no. 3 (2005): 377–91.
de la Fuente, Alejandro. "Race and Inequality in Cuba, 1899–1981." *Journal of Contemporary History* 30, no. 1 (1995): 131–68. doi.org/10.1177/002200949503000106.

Della Paolera, Gerardo, and Alan M. Taylor, eds. *A New Economic History of Argentina*, Volume 1. New York: Cambridge University Press, 2003.
Eltis, David, and David Richardson, eds. *Extending the Frontiers: Essays on the New Transatlantic Slave Trade Database*. New Haven: Yale University Press, 2008.
Haber, Stephen H. "Industrial Concentration and the Capital Markets: A Comparative Study of Brazil, Mexico, and the United States, 1830–1930." *The Journal of Economic History* 51, no. 3 (1991): 559–80.
Haber, Stephen H., ed. *How Latin America Fell Behind: Essays on the Economic Histories of Brazil and Mexico*. Stanford: Stanford University Press, 1997.
Haber, Stephen H. "Financial Market Regulation, Imperfect Capital Markets, and Industrial Concentration: Mexico in Comparative Perspective, 1830–1930." *Economía Mexicana Nueva Época*, volumen VII, número 1, 1er semestre de 1998, pp. 5–46 (1998).
Haber, Stephen H. "The Political Economy of Industrialization." In *The Cambridge Economic History of Latin America. Volume II. The Long Twentieth Century*, edited by Victor Bulmer-Thomas, John H. Coatsworth, and Roberto Cortés Conde, 537–84. New York: Cambridge University Press, 2006.
Hanley, Anne G. *Native Capital: Financial Institutions and Economic Development in São Paulo, Brazil, 1850–1920*. Stanford: Stanford University Press, 2005.
Hatton, T.J., and Jeffrey G. Williamson. *Migration and the International Labor Market, 1850–1939*. London: Routledge, 1994. https://doi.org/10.4324/9780203980163.
Holloway, Thomas H. *Immigrants on the Land: Coffee and Society in São Paulo, 1886–1934*. Chapel Hill: University of North Carolina Press, 1980.
Jacino, Ramatis. *Transição e exclusão: O negro no mercado de trabalho em São Paulo pós abolição-1912/1920*. São Paulo: Editora Nefertiti, 2014.
Marichal, Carlos. "Obstacles to the Development of Capital Markets in Nineteenth-Century Mexico." In *How Latin America Fell Behind: Essays on the Economic Histories of Brazil and Mexico, 1800–1914*, edited by Stephen H. Haber, 118–45. Stanford: Stanford University Press, 1997.
Mitchener, Kris James, and Marc D. Weidenmier. "The Baring Crisis and the Great Latin American Meltdown of the 1890s." *The Journal of Economic History* 68, no. 2 (2008): 462–500.
Musacchio, Aldo. *Experiments in Financial Democracy: Corporate Governance and Financial Development in Brazil, 1882–1950*. Cambridge: Cambridge University Press, 2009.
Rein, Raanan. "Jewish History, Life, and Culture in Latin America." *Latin American Research Review* 49, no. 2 (2014): 253–61.
Salvucci, Richard. "Export-Led Industrialization." In *The Cambridge Economic History of Latin America. Volume II. The Long Twentieth Century*, edited by Victor Bulmer-Thomas, John H. Coatsworth, and Roberto Cortés Conde, 249–92. New York: Cambridge University Press.
Solberg, Carl. "Immigration and Urban Social Problems in Argentina and Chile, 1890–1914." *Hispanic American Historical Review* 49, no. 2 (1969): 215–32.
Stein, Stanley J. *Vassouras, a Brazilian Coffee County, 1850–1900: The Roles of Planter and Slave in a Plantation Society*, Volume 69. Princeton: Princeton University Press, 1985.
Stepan, Nancy. *"The Hour of Eugenics": Race, Gender, and Nation in Latin America*. Ithaca: Cornell University Press, 1991.

Summerhill, William R. *Order Against Progress: Government, Foreign Investment, and Railroads in Brazil, 1854–1913*. Stanford: Stanford University Press, 2003.
Taylor, Alan M. "Argentina and the World Capital Market: Saving, Investment, and International Capital Mobility in the Twentieth Century." *Journal of Development Economics* 57, no. 1 (1998): 147–84.
Topik, Steven, Carlos Marichal, and Zephyr Frank, eds. *From Silver to Cocaine: Latin American Commodity Chains and the Building of the World Economy, 1500–2000*. Durham: Duke University Press, 2006.
Triner, Gail D. "Banks, Regions, and Nation in Brazil, 1889–1930." *Latin American Perspectives* 26, no. 1 (1999): 129–50.
Triner, Gail D., and Kirsten Wandschneider. "The Baring Crisis and the Brazilian Encilhamento, 1889–1891: An Early Example of Contagion among Emerging Capital Markets." *Financial History Review* 12, no. 2 (2005): 199–225.
Truzzi, Oswaldo M.S. "The Right Place at the Right Time: Syrians and Lebanese in Brazil and the United States, a Comparative Approach." *Journal of American Ethnic History* (1997): 3–34.

4 Export-led Growth (1870–1930): Part II

This chapter again uses the production function to better understand how the dynamics of land, labor, capital, and entrepreneurship shaped the export-led growth period of the region's economic history. On the capital and land side of the equation, smaller countries were often unable to finance substantial loans in European capital markets. To connect to global markets, many offered concessions to foreigners and companies like the **United Fruit Company** (UFC) to build similar infrastructure projects that larger countries enjoyed. In the case of the UFC, what started as a railway venture came to include considerable tracts of land effectively controlled by the international conglomerate. Negotiations were often with United States' businessmen and corporations, partially a function of the shared border with Mexico and coastline around the Caribbean Sea. By the onset of World War I, the United States already had significant influence in the circum-Caribbean;[1] the war opened the door to expand further south.

The UFC also serves to highlight an important regional production paradox. Latin American exports wielded considerable influence over economic and political decisions, but 80 percent of national production was for domestic markets. This meant most of the population, the labor side of the production equation, was engaged in largely non-export agricultural production, and increasingly, in the service and industrial sector. However, they did not reap the same benefits as land-holding elites, industrialists, or even laborers employed in the export sector. In Mexico, the tinderbox of persistent inequality, land accumulation, marginalization, combined with political frustration, erupted in the 1910 Mexican Revolution.

Mexican development of the period demonstrates growing disparities, and those available for the region as a whole point to mixed results during the export-led growth period. Cumulatively some advancements were made in terms of education and mortality, but a closer look reveals growing disparities between and within countries. Laborers, workers, and the lower class expressed discontent in the form of strikes, a strategy used with increasing frequency after the onset of World War I. As **Peru's 1919**

DOI: 10.4324/9781003283843-4

General Strike demonstrates, urban workers began to achieve some modest success with labor movements, while most of their rural counterparts continued to face exploitation and strike repression.

United Fruit Company Incorporated, 1899 (Boston, Massachusetts, United States)

In 1870, Costa Rica's President, Tomás Guardia, contracted Minor Keith and his uncle, Henry Meiggs, to build a national railroad from the country's main Caribbean port to its capital, San José. West Indian laborers, mostly Jamaican, were brought in from the Caribbean to complete the back-breaking work. These laborers planted banana trees along the rails: a way of bringing a bit of home with them and of providing additional sustenance. When Keith ran out of money with only 60 miles of rail completed, he also planted bananas, but in the hopes of selling them for profit in New Orleans. There was growing demand for bananas in the United States, a market developed by the Boston Fruit Company selling Jamaican, Cuban, and Dominican bananas in the US northeast. In 1899, indebted due to his railroad venture and in need of a new distributor, Keith merged his operations with Boston Fruit and the United Fruit Company (UFC) was born. At its peak, the UFC operated in Colombia, Panama, Honduras, Guatemala, Costa Rica, the Dominican Republic, Jamaica, and Nicaragua, controlling land that equaled the size of Rhode Island and Connecticut. Within these countries, the UFC banana zones operated as autonomous enclaves with extraordinary political, social, and economic power.

Central American nations, smaller and unable to secure loans as easily as their Southern Cone counterparts, particularly in the wake of the Baring Crisis, negotiated with foreign investors like the UFC. Countries conceded tax breaks, exemptions from port duties, and land concessions to secure railroad and agricultural developers' interest. Minor Keith, for example, received 800,000 acres of tax-free land from Costa Rica to develop the railroad. In turn, companies provided vital infrastructure that countries were unable to provide otherwise. At incorporation, the UFC operated just 112 railway miles. By 1930, it operated over 1,700 miles. Infrastructure went well beyond rails: in Guatemala the UFC began running the country's postal service in 1901 and the Tropical Radio & Telegraph service in 1913.

The company's rise demonstrates the United States' increasing economic role in Latin America. By the start of World War I the United States had already invested $1.2 billion into the region. Collectively, Mexico and Central America and the Caribbean accounted for 79 percent of these investments.[2] Most funds poured into transportation oriented toward the export sector, such as railroads. Export priorities often dictated where new track lines would be laid, leaving portions of the population with minimal or no access to transportation developments. In 1877, Mexico counted just 400 miles of track in service that linked Mexico City to the Caribbean port of Veracruz. When Porfirio Díaz came to power in 1876, his autocratic ruling brought the stability that US investors craved. By 1891, the Mexican National Railway was completed, linking Mexico City directly to Corpus Christi, Texas almost in a straight line.

US capital also played a deciding role in developing ports and fluvial transport. In the midst of Colombia's War of a Thousand Days (1899–1902), a civil conflict between liberals and conservatives that left 70,000 dead and no clear victor, the United States turned its attention to Colombia's northernmost province of Panama. The isthmus was disconnected from much of Colombia's capital both geographically and socially, but as the narrowest point in the hemisphere it offered the best chance for a canal to link the Atlantic Ocean and Caribbean to the Pacific Ocean. After Colombia's Senate rejected a treaty that would have ceded control to the United States of a Canal Zone for 99 years, the US threw support behind Panamanian rebels and promptly recognized Panama's independence. Panama ceded control of the Canal Zone to the US government in 1903, and a combination of railroad, engineering, and army leaders oversaw the construction. They used what they could of the infrastructure left behind by a failed French endeavor to create the canal, bringing in Spanish, Black West Indians, and Black Americans to complete construction. To build the canal "the North Americans invested 352 million dollars and ended with a balance in human lives of 5,609 people [dead], of whom 4,500 were black workers."[3] There were countless others like Wilfred McDonald, a widower who, having lost both his legs in construction, had no means to raise his two children.[4]

Investments in the Caribbean translated to considerable interference in national sovereignty and fiscal policy in the interest of protecting US businesses. The most enduring interference came with the occupation of Puerto Rico in the wake of the 1898 Spanish-American War. Puerto Rico became "a territory … belonging to the United States, but not a part of the United States."[5] While in 1952 it became a Commonwealth, it still occupies a liminal status. Cuba gained independence during the war, but US occupations in 1905–1909 and 1917–1921 also impeded sovereignty. The situation was not much different on adjacent Hispaniola. Neither Haiti nor the Dominican Republic had gained political stability enjoyed by most of mainland Latin America. Between the 1840s and 1910, 21 of 22 Haitian presidents were assassinated and between 1911 and 1915 alone, there were six presidential changes. The Dominican Republic was no better, counting 30 revolutions and 50 presidents from the 1840s to 1930s. With such uncertainty used as justification, the United States occupied Haiti during 1915–1934 and the Dominican Republic during 1916–1924. As part of the occupation, the US assumed control of Haiti's National Treasury and Bank, using 40 percent of Haiti's national income to finance foreign debt (predominantly US and German). In the Dominican Republic, US occupation skewed the economy toward lucrative sugar production. A similar dynamic developed in Nicaragua, where loans to the country came with two considerable concessions. First, in order to ensure that customs duties were directed toward debt payments, the Nicaraguan customs collector would be nominated by US bankers and approved by the United States Secretary of State before being appointed by Nicaragua's president. Second, the Nicaragua National Bank was created. However, it was to be incorporated in the United States and a majority of shareholders would be US bankers. This interference was the rule, not the exception: 10 out of 20 Latin American republics had US officials in some form of supervising capacity in customs offices to make sure that debts were being serviced.[6]

With a significant foothold in the Caribbean, Central American, and Mexican economies through both government intervention and private investment, the United States accelerated its role in Latin America during and after World War I. War-torn Europe, now more occupied with rebuilding the continent, was unable to invest to the same degree. This created an environment that switched the political and economic power dynamics. By 1929, US investment in the region had more than tripled, making it the biggest lender. In the post-war era US interests ventured further south: South America now accounted for 56 percent of US investments in the region.

The UFC was an outlier in the scale of its venture and influence, but its approach to Latin America's export market conforms to a general trend toward great land accumulation. Already steeped in colonial practices of unequal land distribution, as individuals and companies bought and secured land concessions, Latin America took further steps to becoming the region in the world with the highest land inequality. In Mexico, for example, mid-nineteenth-century liberal reforms opened lands formerly under the Catholic Church's domain and, along with railroads, facilitated further expropriation of Indigenous lands. Established landowners added to their holdings by purchasing and appropriating land. By 1910, half of Mexico's land was controlled by just 1 percent of the population, leaving 97 percent of Mexicans landless. In the silver-rich Zacatecas region, eight haciendas extended over 100,000 hectares. Many landowners were not foreigners like the UFC, but rather national elites or individuals benefiting from **patronage** *networks that rewarded loyalty and social connections rather than aptitude.* There were some instances of small and medium land holders gaining a foothold, such as in central Mexico or the Argentine pampas, but these were the exception. By the end of the period, Latin

American land distribution was considerably more unequal than both developed and undeveloped parts of the world.

The scale of accumulation would have been impossible without railroad expansion. Prior to railroads, with few navigable rivers in the region, the most reliable method of transport was via mules or pack animals. Railways, thus, brought higher cost savings to Latin America than they did to the United States by expanding production of agricultural products into new frontiers and making transport more reliable and cheaper. Exports flourished, like coffee in Brazil and Colombia, and nitrates and copper in Chile, but the domestic market also expanded. Railroads *made new ventures possible, including agriculture for domestic consumption, services, and new industries*. These are known as **forward linkages. Backward linkages,** however, were slow to develop when they developed at all. *New sectors needed to produce and create the inputs* for railways, such as train car construction or steel, rarely materialized, forcing countries and companies to spend railway revenues importing nails, tools, and equipment. Even when domestic iron and steel production developed, as was the case in Mexico, it did not cut down significantly on imported dependence on foreign iron and steel.

The UFC itself profited considerably from forward linkages, becoming the pinnacle of vertical integration. It expanded banana enterprises in new countries and acquired competing banana importers, growing horizontally, but it also expanded into cacao and sugar production. Those bananas it did not produce it acquired from local growers, effectively making the UFC a monopsony, or the sole buyer in most countries. Acquiring and funding companies connected to supporting exporting tropical agriculture production, like shipping, railroads, and communication, typified its vertical expansion (see Figure 4.1). The UFC operated 24 radio stations (only

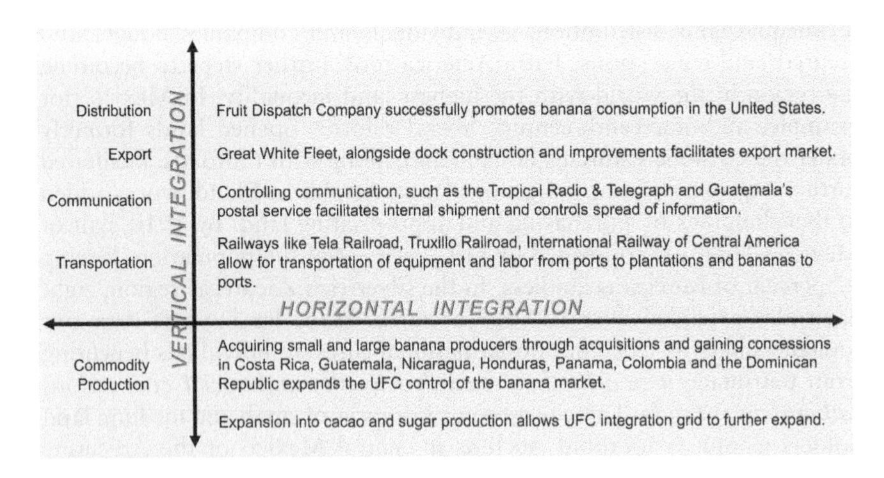

Figure 4.1 Vertical and horizontal integration at the United Fruit Company (UFC).

five of which were company-specific) that broadcast beyond the banana enclaves and developed docks and fluvial transportation with its Great White Fleet, a commercial and passenger shipping company.

Railroad expansion also brought renewed vigor to centuries-old conflicts over Indigenous lands, further eroding pre-colonial communal landholding practices that had survived in some parts of the region. In 1854, roughly 5,000 independent Indigenous communities existed in Mexico, but the 1883 Land Law jeopardized these groups. If individuals or communal land holders could not produce a land title, the land reverted to the government, where it could be given as a concession. Between 1880 and 1900, 134 million acres reverted to the state and by 1910, more than 95 percent of Mexico's rural population worked as *hacienda* laborers. In northern Mexico, after defeating the Yaqui Indians, Mexico gave the Los Angeles Richardson Construction Company a land grant roughly a quarter the size of El Salvador. The Yaquis were just one of many Indigenous groups whose culture and language encountered significant challenges in the face of export-oriented growth. Similar conflicts with the Botacudo in Brazil and the Mapuche in Chile were aggravated by agricultural expansion. Even when the process was more gradual, communal land practices had largely eroded by the end of the export-oriented period in 1930.

Was there an economic reasoning to justify such incredible accumulation? The **economies of scale** argument, or the idea that only *through large-scale production could a venture be possible or profitable*, does not explain land accumulation in areas where small and medium landholdings were also profitable. Small-scale production was cost-prohibitive only in the case of sugar, and arguably bananas. With these products, larger enterprises prevented products from spoiling, but coffee, cacao, and wheat, for example, could be just as profitable through small and medium land holding.[7] Furthermore, outside of the Southern Cone and Cuba, while 70 percent of Latin America's economically active population was employed in agriculture, only 20 percent of agricultural production was devoted to export products. Most landowners, and thus tenant farmers and rural laborers, produced goods for the domestic market. A dualistic agricultural system developed. For the 20 percent of land devoted to exports, new technologies were implemented, and efficiency, profitability, and, at times, wages increased. For the non-export agricultural sectors, costs and preferences saw agriculturalists fail to implement new agricultural technology, often relying on colonial technologies and practices that impeded greater efficiency.

Under such accumulation in a land-abundant space, Latin American wages largely failed to rise to the expected levels. The region had an abundance of land relative to its population: even after mass immigration, Brazil and Argentina averaged just three people living in every square kilometer in 1913. Even the most densely populated countries, El Salvador and Haiti, averaged just 70 people living per square kilometer. Theoretically, under these conditions, as labor demands grew (as they did during the period of export-oriented growth), owners could entice tenant farmers, *campesinos*, daily agricultural, and daily laborers with higher wages and better conditions. In another scenario, if owners wanted to keep labor costs low, they could invest more in technological and agricultural advances to limit their labor needs. In this scenario, displaced workers would likely move to urban centers. An alternative method to keep wages low, however, was to exploit local and migratory labor and to create artificial labor shortages.

Unfortunately for Latin America's development, the labor exploitation often outweighed higher wages, better conditions, and technological advancement. This tendency aligned with colonial labor exploitation and the persistence of slavery through 1888. Evidence of increasing agricultural wages in export-oriented regions, such as Southeastern Brazil, Argentina's Pampas, and southern Mexico lend some support to the predicted higher wages. Mine workers also received somewhat higher wages, but often had to buy overpriced items at company stores. Some immigration strategies even enticed immigrants with land ownership. There was also some improvement in implementing technology. In the Southern Cone, non-export commerce benefited from the technological advancements of the export market and urbanization and industrial diversification ensued. Some Mexican commercial farmers also implemented new technologies for the domestic market, but investments in agricultural technology remained low and gains in non-export sectors were underwhelming. Most landowners opted to keep wage costs low by relying more heavily on labor exploitation rather than technological improvements. Such was the case for Mayan laborers in southern Mexico's henequen plantations, Brazil's Amazon rubber plantations, and areas of Peru, Bolivia, Colombia, and Guatemala. This was also the case for many agricultural laborers, producing foodstuff for domestic markets.

Presumably, with more export revenues generated during this phase, national governments could invest in social services for the broad population. By 1930, some gains had been made in terms of health and education. The average life expectancy increased by three years between 1910 and 1930, illiteracy declined by 10 percent in the same period, and numeracy had reached almost 90 percent by the end of the period. Average schooling also increased from less than a year in 1870 to almost 2.3 years in 1930. But, as scholars have found this to be a period of increasing inequality within the region and within individual countries, equal access to those gains was lagging. Even in Southern Cone countries, where GDP per capita figures grew closer to European and US figures, internal inequality grew. Wages declined relative to both land prices and GDP per capita, meaning that even when land became more valuable and countries became wealthier relative to other countries, that new wealth did not reach the typical worker. Research on changes in average heights corroborate a period of hardship, as well as expanding national disparities. *When children do not receive adequate nutrition or suffer from health challenges, they often have below-average heights*, an effect known as **stunting**. Reduced heights thus are often a sign of underdevelopment. In Argentina, residents in the Pampas region, the center of Argentina's export sector, were significantly taller than their interior counterparts. In Brazil, northeasterners lagged behind other regions, particularly the southeast coffee-growing region. In Argentina, urban professionals and students grew taller much faster than unskilled laborers. A similar effect occurred in Mexico and Brazil where middle-class passport holders grew to average height, whereas lower-class military recruits either experienced a reversal, or only gained minimally in stature. More research into other countries' heights and standards of living will likely yield similar trends.

The Mexican Revolution stands as a cautionary tale of the costs such inequities present. Under Porfírio Díaz's presidency and 34 years of relative political stability, railroad and industrial growth had also pushed many Mexicans to the brink. Even prior to Díaz's ascendancy to the presidency in 1876, most Mexicans experienced declining living standards. By the early twentieth century, a growing urban middle class and professionals were tired of undemocratic elections and Díaz's *científicos*, hand-picked technocrats, disproportionately benefiting from the country's growing economy. The economic downturn in 1907 brought matters to a head. Over 100 strikes occurred between 1905 and 1910. Striking Cananea Copper Company miners (1906) and Rio Branco textile workers (1907), discontented with company stores and low wages, faced violent repression under the Díaz regime. When Díaz once again ran for the presidency in 1910, the country erupted. Northern workers and southern agricultural laborers provided the bulk of the man- (and woman-) power behind the civil conflict. While the rest of the region felt the challenges of World War I, Mexico endured self-inflicted violence between 1913 and 1917. Ten percent of Mexico's population died in the Revolution.[8] Many foreign skilled workers also left, resulting in a dearth of technical knowledge. While industrial imports rebounded relatively quickly, agricultural production only returned to pre-Revolution levels between 1934 and 1940.

A semblance of peace arrived with the 1917 Constitution, but in some areas, fighting persisted through the 1920s. Among other revolutionary reforms, the constitution called for **agrarian reform**, *a restructuring of the existing land ownership structure that would be redistributive in nature*. Mexico's reform maximized private property lots at 100 hectares and reinstituted communal land practices through the *ejido* grants.[9] It would not be until the Cárdenas era of the 1930s that many of these agricultural reforms came to fruition, but the first steps had been taken with the Constitution and it served as a harbinger of the political jockeying that would be required in the state-led industrialization period that followed.

Agricultural labor dissatisfaction also mounted within the UFC banana zones of Central America. The workforce in these zones included contracted skilled and unskilled workers, creating parallel cultural communities. Engineers and executives enjoyed US-style houses and lawns while laborers created and relied on mutual aid societies and churches for social supports. World War I challenged the system: many commodity prices fell, including banana prices. Worldwide deflation in 1920 and 1921 compounded the problem with commodity prices falling even further. The lucrative banana industry had done little to reduce structural inequalities in the region. When the UFC implemented cost-saving measures, workers often suffered. Facing deteriorating conditions, UFC workers formed unions in Honduras and Guatemala in the 1920s. When Cuyamel Fruit banana workers in Nicaragua went on strike in 1925, they faced heavy repression.[10] By 1926, workers in Santa Marta, Colombia reached their tipping point, forming the Unionist Unity of Workers of Magdalena (USTM). Workers went on strike in 1928. In response, the United Fruit Company called on the Colombian government's armed forces, which arrested strikers, and on December 5, "the soldiers fired into massed crowds, killing hundreds."[11] The strike was effectively repressed, but it remained an indelible mark in campaigns for change and reform. Colombian Nobel Prize–winning author Gabriel García Márquez even enshrined the struggle, as well as the impact of railroads on a fictional community, in his 1967 allegorical masterpiece, *One Hundred Years of Solitude.*

Lima General Strike, 1919 (Lima, Peru)

In Peru, legislation passed in 1918 restricted workdays for women and children to eight hours. The impact in textiles was considerable as women and children comprised a sizeable portion of the sector's labor force. Overall production fell up to 20 percent, and for families whose households relied on women's and children's wages, the reduction created a precarious situation. In protest, weavers went on strike in December of 1918. By January 13, 1919, it became a general strike with workers in Lima and in the nearby port of Callao striking for a general eight-hour workday. The weavers who started the strike did not even earn hourly wages, being paid a piece rate, so while they fought for an eight-hour workday, they also demanded an increase in piece rates to compensate for the income lost by reduced work hours. Stevedores provided a physical incentive not to be strikebreakers and the fact that urban transport was also on strike made it difficult to find replacement workers. *Limeños* at large were impacted:

striking bakers created a bread shortage and there was even a run on foodstuffs in anticipation of stores closing and supply shortages from striking dockworkers.[12] After just two days, President Pardo ceded the eight-hour workday that laborers demanded. Ironically, workers failed to gain wage or piece rate increases, the original demand of weavers, demonstrating the complex nature of labor organization.

Both the 1919 Lima General Strike and Colombia's 1928 Magdalena Strike reflect Latin American labor and working-class organization during this period of export-oriented growth. Agricultural laborers were often directly connected to the export sector, but industrial workers were also indirectly connected. As industry grew, so too did labor organization. Strikes, however, concentrated in two periods, 1902–1908 and 1917–1921. They were also more common in urban spaces, especially between 1900 and 1930, of which Peru's 1919 General Strike stands as just one example. Organization tended to be more successful in cities, where a growing middle class sometimes supported organization and strikers could effectively paralyze domestic industrial production and the domestic economy.

Conditions did not necessarily improve in the 1920s, but growing labor discontent in the post-war era created an environment where employers took into account labor conditions and politicians began incorporating working-class concerns into political platforms. Male workers represented an expanding voting bloc. To understand what motivated laborers in this moment requires understanding changing standards of living. In urban centers, this means exploring industrial growth during the period and examining how laborers and industrialists dealt with broader challenges. These included global financial crises, demographic pressures, wartime shortages, and post-war competition. Lima's 1919 General Strike serves as just one example.

Railroads and domestic demand sparked manufacturers to develop. New sectors expanded in products adjacent to the export market or railroads, such as jute sacks (Brazil) or steel mills (Mexico), but then expanded into other finished products like textiles, beer, and cigarettes. Transportation improvements cut production costs, making Latin American products more competitive. Depreciating exchange rates also encouraged domestic industry: imports were more expensive, making cheaper domestic alternatives more attractive to consumers. As these sectors grew, industrialists pressured governments to *increase import tariffs on finished products that competed with national producers*, like textiles and beverages. Simultaneously, they lobbied to keep *tariffs low on production inputs, capital and intermediate goods like machinery and bottles, needed for those finished goods*. The result was ad hoc **trade protection**: by the start of World War I, Latin America's tariff rates were the highest in the world.[13]

These companies and related ventures and services employed a growing number of people living in Latin America. Many of the engineers, highest skilled workers, and some mechanics employed in the companies were foreign workers, but most of the rank-and-file or employees at repair and mechanic shops that developed to service machinery and vehicles were national workers. Rags to riches stories were few and far between, but for men who did not face discriminatory hiring practices, industrial companies could offer the chance for social mobility into higher skilled manual labor.

By the start of World War I, all countries had an industrial sector to speak of, and one that through tariffs had created some level of trade protection for Latin American manufactures. In Argentina, Brazil, Chile, Mexico, Peru, and Uruguay, domestic production accounted for 50 to 80 percent of domestic consumption. This did not necessarily mean that domestic production matched imported quality. As one Portuguese immigrant wrote to his wife about to join him in Brazil, she needed to make sure to bring hats, shoes, and even socks, as he was outraged at paying a high price for socks that developed a hole in just four-hour's time.[14]

The growing industrial sector also meant a growing industrial workforce and increased urbanization. In 1913, just 11 percent of the region's population lived in cities. But in Argentina and Uruguay, the rate was closer to 30, and Chile, Paraguay, and Cuba hovered around 15 percent. By 1930, average urbanization rates in the region reached 30 percent, and were above 50 percent in Argentina, Chile, Uruguay, and Cuba. Jobs were not the only draw to urban centers: services concentrated in cities and service economies, from theaters and movie houses to tailors and repair shops, developed to satisfy the local resident demands. Mutual aid societies proliferated along professional and ethnic lines, providing members social, moral, and economic support in times of prosperity and duress alike.

Urban residents also sought out education for their children, and it was during this period that Latin American education began to expand. The biggest boon to education came through increasing export revenues, which directed more money toward public education.[15] Literacy rates and enrollment rates show that progress finally began, with half of the school-aged population enrolled in Argentina, Chile, Colombia, Costa Rica, Uruguay, Mexico, and Panama, and literacy rates reaching 50 percent for the entire region by 1930. Uruguay and Argentina led the way, with literacy rates reaching 75 percent by 1920. This progress was extended to girls and boys alike. Female primary school enrollment rates were 45 percent by 1930, a level well above levels for Asia, the Middle East, and Africa.

Latin America still lagged well behind most of Europe and the United States, with enrollments lower than expected based on the region's GDP per capita. Educational gains concentrated among urban residents and their children where large, school-age populations required official attention. This was true even in Argentina and Uruguay. Normal schools for teacher training were also centered in cities, meaning not only a difference in quantity but also in quality of instruction in urban as opposed to rural areas. Educational achievements, thus, often failed or lagged significantly in reaching populations in rural areas, where the majority of Latin America's population still lived.

Alongside educational resources, urban and state officials, often operating on limited budgets subject to export product price fluctuations, struggled to provide housing and other social services. In this environment, working-class entrepreneurship and informality flourished. To deal with housing shortages, owners and tenants sublet rooms and even beds, bringing in additional income. When geographies permitted, constructing unregulated houses in urban peripheries became a weekend pastime. In Brazil, officials struggled to control the (illegal) *jogo do bicho* lottery based on the Rio de Janeiro zoo's featured animal of the day, but local vendors benefited from the additional income. Unlicensed street vendors overwhelmed officials and fee-paying market vendors alike, but they could provide a valuable service, bringing merchandise closer to consumers. Unregulated housing and commerce came at a cost. Disease proliferated in overcrowded accommodations and consumers complained of watered-down or adulterated products. Death by spoiled meat was a veritable concern. Overwhelmed by market volatility and urban populations, it is in this period that much **informality**, *unregulated activity and space*, prominent in Latin American societies later in the twentieth century, became entrenched in daily practices.

Informality demonstrates just one of the challenges that came with urbanization. Nutrition suffered and overcrowding and disease were other constant concerns. Where we have information on average heights, there seems to be some variance within Latin America as to whether the city or the countryside was a healthier environment. In Mexico, urban workers tended to be taller than rural laborers, but both saw heights fall between 1850 and 1930. Argentina saw a similar decline between 1900 and 1913 among army recruits. Brazilians, on the other hand, seemed to get taller beginning in 1870, but the period between 1880 and 1910 demonstrated the potential costs of living in a city: urban military recruits were shorter than their rural counterparts.

Discontent simmered just below the surface when jobs were readily available, but coalesced when demographic pressure, exchange rates, or production reductions saw **real wages** and incomes decline. When consumer *income declined relative to inflation, reducing the value of what people could purchase*, strikes and labor organization increased. In countries that had developed a sizeable industrial sector, this occurred between 1902 and 1908. In the Southern Cone, the constant arrival of new immigrants increased job competition, keeping wages low and creating a housing crisis. In Mexico, the United States' financial crisis of 1907 created a recession; by restricting foreign investments into the country, Mexico's economy contracted. Industrialists responded by importing less machinery and cutting work hours. The result: 125 separate strikes between 1905 and 1910. Labor was slower to organize in the Caribbean islands and Nicaragua, areas with direct United States intervention and smaller economies, but even here, mutual aid societies gained a foothold in the first decade of the twentieth century.

While an eight-hour workday and higher wages were chief rallying points, mobilizing extended beyond labor conditions. Neighborhood committees organized to improve living conditions and standards of living. In 1907, 10 percent of Buenos Aires residents refused to pay rents. Women took an active role, withholding payment, advocating for neighbors facing eviction, and even speaking at rallies. Neighborhood committees in Chile led a protest to eliminate import tariffs on Argentine beef in 1905, an effort to reduce substantial increases in food costs. After police attacked restless protestors, Santiago broke out in violence and looting, revealing the substantial class differences in Chile's urban society. These rallying points demonstrate notable female participation in early movements particularly concerning issues adjacent to wage and labor conditions.

Interest in female labor force participation in Latin America since the 1960s garners much attention, but census records also show sizeable female participation in the early twentieth century. In the absence of enforceable labor laws and with the often-temporary nature of employment, women comprised upwards of 40 percent of the urban workforce in some Latin American cities.[16] Women received lower wages than men for the same jobs, making them an attractive alternative for industrialists trying to minimize labor costs. They concentrated in service positions and made up the majority of textile workers, but women also worked in other sectors. In Chile, for example, women worked as tram operators. Female labor participation was even greater if we look beyond the formal labor market. Unofficially, women often took in additional washing and piece-rate work like embroidery or lacework to supplement household income.

The challenges of World War I (and the Mexican Revolution in the case of that country) saw conditions worsen for most of the urban working class. While some exports like copper, nitrates, and rubber increased substantially during the war, most of Latin America's exports lost value in the global market, straining national budgets. The lack of imported machinery and European and American finished products compounded matters, initiating supply shortages and production challenges. Some countries expanded production in sectors of consumer products, like textiles and shoes, but increased production did not come with better work conditions. Workers increasingly struggled to put food on the table as prices increased faster than wages. Coupled with the Russian Revolution (1917–1921), Latin America saw increased labor mobilization between 1917 and 1919.

Conditions did not improve much after the end of World War I. In some ways they were worse: one to two years into the Spanish flu pandemic, which began in 1918, facing competition from European goods that had returned to Latin American markets, unemployment and underemployment were high. Even if workers were employed fulltime, their purchasing power was far lower than it had been prior to World War I. Here was the worker paradox: workers wanted higher wages to address the rising cost of living, but as consumers, they also demanded lower costs, which jeopardized their own jobs. Faced with these challenges, industrialists lobbied for high import tariffs on final products, but low or minimal tariffs on imported machinery and inputs. Workers returned to labor organization with renewed vigor.

From Honduras to Paraguay and Argentina to Colombia, the region witnessed a series of strikes, including general strikes, that disrupted industrial production. The formula for a general strike was consistent: discontent and organization at a major factory met with a police presence. In the aftermath of conflict between strikers and police, and in some cases the armed forces, workers at other companies and in other sectors rallied together. While the male role is often emphasized in these movements, women were active participants and instigators at this stage of the organization. After strikes expanded across sectors, strike leaders rose to the front in these moments to coalesce general strikes. While these leaders were often in some way connected to European anarcho-syndicalists or with some intention of continuing Russia's 1917 Bolshevik Revolution, most rank and file were not radicalized; they were men and women trying to provide for their families. Facing such disruption to the domestic market, negotiations eventually occurred, or some concessions were made to strikers.

Peru's general strike was resolved with minimal disturbance to social order, but in other cities general strikes could stretch on for weeks and could be more dramatic. Such was the case in Buenos Aires, Argentina. The *semana trágica* in January 1919 left hundreds killed or wounded and included an ethno-religious attack of Argentina's Russian-Jewish population. In the chaos and clashes between labor organizers, vigilantes, and police that erupted in the wake of a metalworkers' strike, they were falsely accused of instigating a Bolshevik plot.

Ten years before Colombia's Magdalena Strike, which was easily thwarted in 1928 partially due to its rural setting, massive urban strikes could shut down entire countries' industrial sectors. Add to the mix the support of a small but growing middle class, as well as some industrial elites dissatisfied with the political status quo dominated by agriculture, and these strikes had the potential to effect change. While workday and wage concessions were often short-lived or eliminated by inflation, these strikes marked a shift in the relative bargaining power of labor and working-class concerns. By the end of the export-oriented growth period, industrialists were more willing to consider working conditions in the interest of stability and predictability. Politicians began to take notice of the potential voting power of urban workers, making way for proto-populist and populist political leaders that emerged in the subsequent period of state-led industrialization (1930–1979).

Notes

1 The circum-Caribbean refers to both independent island and continental nations with a Caribbean border.
2 Mexico and Central America made up 57 percent and the Caribbean 20 percent, Bulmer-Thomas, *Economic History of Latin America*, 3rd edition, p. 158.
3 Fernandez and Marcos, "El Canal de Panamá."
4 Lifers, "How the Panama Canal Took a Huge Toll."
5 The Foraker Act, Public Law 56–191, signed into law by President McKinley on April 12, 1900.
6 Bulmer-Thomas, *Economic History of Latin America* 3rd edition, p. 195.
7 Lurtz, *From the Grounds Up*, shows this to be the case for coffee growers in southern Mexico and Guatemala.
8 Another 10 percent of the population moved to the United States between 1900 and 1929, the years of increasing economic hardship through the Cristero War, 1926–1929, García, *Mexicans in the Midwest*.
9 *Ejidos* were communal, pre-colonial land ownership practices, but a growing population made *ejidos* untenable. They were too small to compete with larger producers and became increasingly smaller, preventing even subsistence farming (see Solbrig, "Structure, Performance and Policy in Agriculture," pp. 524–27).
10 Cuyamel Fruit was sold to the United Fruit Company in the wake of the Great Depression.
11 Pedraja Tomán, "Colombia," p. 202.
12 *El Deber* [07 January 1919], British Library, EAP726/1/1/30/5; *El Deber* [13 January 1919], British Library, EAP726/1/1/30/10.
13 The tariff rates in the largest economies were five times higher than in Western Europe and an order of magnitude higher than in East Asian countries (Haber, "The Political Economy," p. 548, citing Coatsworth and Williamson).
14 Arquivo Distrital do Porto, Processos de passaporte, cx.0136, nº337.
15 Although total spending did increase, nominal spending and educational spending per capita made minimal advancements.
16 Women represented 39 percent of the workforce of Buenos Aires, 35 percent in Santiago and Valparaíso in Chile, and 33 percent of Brazil's industrial labor force in 1920 (Korzeniewicz, "Labor Unrest in Argentina, 1887–1907"; De Shazo, *Urban Workers and Labor Unions in Chile, 1902–1927*; Ribeiro, *Condições de trabalho na indústria têxtil paulista (1870–1930)*).

Suggested Media, Literature, and Digital Resources

García Márquez, Gabriel. *One Hundred Years of Solitude*. Translated by Gregory Rabassa. New York: Harper Perennial Modern Classics, 2006.
"Latin American Newspapers Database, series 1 and 2." Readex: Newsbank. Accessed July 14, 2023. https://www.readex.com/products/latin-american-newspapers-series-1-and-2-1805-1922.

"Preserving Peruvian Newspapers for a Regional Approach: Key 19th–20th Century Press in Arequipa." British Library Endangered Archives Programme. Accessed July 25, 2023. https://doi.org/10.15130/EAP726.

"United Fruit Company Photographs." Harvard Library. https://library.harvard.edu/collections/united-fruit-company-photographs.

Select Bibliography

Adams, Frederick Upham. *Conquest of the Tropics: The Story of the Creative Enterprises Conducted by the United Fruit Company*. Garden City: Doubleday, Page & Company, 1914.

Baer, James A. "Tenant Mobilization and the 1907 Rent Strike in Buenos Aires." *The Americas* 49, no. 3 (1993): 343–68. doi:10.2307/1007030.

Bucheli, Marcelo, and Ian Read. "Banana Boats and Baby Food: The Banana in US History." In *World Economy, 1500–2000*, 204–27. Durham: Duke University Press, 2006.

Bucheli, Marcelo. *Bananas and Business: The United Fruit Company in Colombia, 1899–2000*. London: University Press, 2005. https://doi.org/10.18574/978147983.

Cerda Castro, Karelia, and Damián Lo Chávez. "Del mutualismo al Centro Femenino Anticlerical Belén de Sárraga: trayectoria de la participación sociopolítica de mujeres en Iquique (1890–1918)." *Revista de Historia (Concepción)* 28, no. 1 (2021): 289–318.

Challú, Amílcar E., and Aurora Gómez-Galvarriato. "Mexico's Real Wages in the Age of the Great Divergence, 1730–1930." *Revista de Historia Económica – Journal of Iberian and Latin American Economic History* 33, no. 1 (2015): 83–122.

Chomsky, Avi. "Afro-Jamaican Traditions and Labor Organizing on United Fruit Company Plantations in Costa Rica, 1910." *Journal of Social History* (1995): 837–55.

De la Pedraja Tomán, René. "Colombia." In *Latin American Labor Organizations*, edited by Gerald Michael Greenfield and Sheldon L. Maram, 179–212. New York: Greenwood Press, 1987.

De Shazo, Peter Charles. *Urban Workers and Labor Unions in Chile, 1902–1927*. Madison: The University of Wisconsin-Madison Press, 1977.

Dye, Alan. *Cuban Sugar in the Age of Mass Production: Technology and the Economics of the Sugar Central, 1899–1929*. Stanford: Stanford University Press, 1998.

Farnsworth-Alvear, Ann. *Dulcinea in the Factory: Myths, Morals, Men, and Women in Colombia's Industrial Experiment, 1905–1960*. Durham: Duke University Press, 2000.

Fernandez, M.A., and J. Marcos. "El canal de Panamá: Una historia repetida de intereses y sobrecostes." *Público*, January 19, 2014. Accessed July 2, 2022. https://www.publico.es/internacional/canal-panama-historia-repetida-intereses.html.

Frankema, Ewout. *Has Latin America Always Been Unequal? A Comparative Study of Asset and Income Inequality in the Long Twentieth Century*, Volume 3. Leiden: Brill, 2009.

Franken, Daniel. "Anthropometric History of Brazil, 1850–1950: Insights from Military and Passport Records." *Revista De Historia Económica – Journal of Iberian and Latin American Economic History* 37, no. 2 (2019): 377–408.

García, Juan R. *Mexicans in the Midwest, 1900–1932*. Tucson: University of Arizona Press, 1996.

Haber, Stephen H. "The Political Economy." In *How Latin America Fell Behind: Essays on the Economic Histories of Brazil and Mexico, 1800–1914*. Stanford: Stanford University Press, 1997.

Korzeniewicz, Roberto P. "Labor Unrest in Argentina, 1887–1907." *Latin American Research Review* 24, no. 3 (1989): 71–98.

LaRosa, Michael J., and Germán R. Mejía. *Colombia: A Concise Contemporary History*. Plymouth: Rowman & Littlefield, 2017.

Lifers, C. "How the Panama Canal Took a Huge Toll on the Contract Workers Who Built It." Smithsonian.com, April 18, 2018. Accessed July 2, 2022.

Lindert, Peter H. "The Unequal Lag in Latin American Schooling Since 1900: Follow the Money." *Revista de Historia Económica – Journal of Iberian and Latin American Economic History* 28, no. 2 (2010): 375–405.

López-Alonso, Moramay. *Measuring Up a History of Living Standards in Mexico, 1850–1950*. Stanford: Stanford University Press, 2012. https://doi.org/10.1515/9780804782852.

Luna, Francisco Vidal, and Herbert S. Klein. *The Economic and Social History of Brazil since 1889*. Cambridge: Cambridge University Press, 2014.

Lurtz, Casey Marina. *From the Grounds Up: Building an Export Economy in Southern Mexico*. Stanford: Stanford University Press, 2019.

Mirelman, Victor A. "The Semana Trágica of 1919 and the Jews in Argentina." *Jewish Social Studies* 37, no. 1 (1975): 67–73.

Pandolfe, Frank C. "The Role of the United States in Nicaragua from 1912–1933." *Fletcher F.* 9 (1985): 401.

Piccato, Pablo. *City of Suspects: Crime in Mexico City, 1900–1931*. Durham: Duke University Press, 2001.

Ribeiro, Maria Alice Rosa. *Condições de trabalho na indústria têxtil paulista (1870–1930)*. São Paulo: Hucitec, 1988.

Salvatore, Ricardo D., Carlos Aguirre, and Gilbert M. Joseph, eds. *Crime and Punishment in Latin America: Law and Society Since Late Colonial Times*. Durham: Duke University Press, 2001.

Schoonover, Thomas D. *The United States in Central America, 1860–1911: Episodes of Social Imperialism and Imperial Rivalry in the World System*. Durham: Duke University Press, 1991.

Solbrig, Otto. "Economic Growth and Environmental Change." In *The Cambridge Economic History of Latin America. Volume II. The Long Twentieth Century*, edited by Victor Bulmer-Thomas, John Coatsworth, and Roberto Cortes-Conde, 329–76. New York: Cambridge University Press, 2006.

———. "Structure, Performance and Policy in Agriculture." In *The Cambridge Economic History of Latin America. Volume II. The Long Twentieth Century*, edited by Victor Bulmer-Thomas, John Coatsworth, and Roberto Cortes-Conde, 483–536. New York: Cambridge University Press, 2006.

Striffler, Steve, and Mark Moberg, eds. *Banana Wars: Power, Production, and History in the Americas*. Durham: Duke University Press, 2003.

Wolfe, Joel. "Anarchist Ideology, Worker Practice: The 1917 General Strike and the Formation of São Paulo's Working Class." *Hispanic American Historical Review* 71, no. 4 (1991): 809–46.

5 State-led Growth (1930–1980)

Over the course of the state-led growth period, government oversight and involvement in national economies increased substantially and Latin America embraced inward-looking development strategies. To a certain degree, this transition away from an export-led growth path kept in line with global tendencies. Protectionist policies became more prominent in the post–World War I era. As the United States and Western Europe struggled to emerge from the Great Depression in the 1930s, governments embraced Keynesian economics, in which government spending played a critical role in jumpstarting and regulating the economy.

The role of the state in the Latin American model, however, continued to grow substantially after World War II as it attempted to confront global and regional structural inequities. This chapter traces that process, from the ad hoc nature of state-led growth during the **Great Depression** to the deliberate tactics introduced by the **Economic Commission for Latin America** starting in the 1950s. Unable to appreciate the behemoth that state-led growth could create, countries often doubled down on the state-led model. By the end of the period, this model also included debt-led growth and a combination of state-owned enterprises and multinational corporations operating throughout the region. While the state-led model had various iterations, most encouraged regional integration, industrialization, and agricultural diversification. Economic growth was consistent during the period of state-led growth, but it was most impressive between 1950 and 1980, growing 2.7 percent per capita annually.

Despite notable growth rates, the inward-looking approach had extreme deficiencies. This chapter also explores how and why internal structural inequalities persisted. The discussion of the **Cuban Revolution** demonstrates the scale of discontent among the broad population, and how entangled economic and hemispheric politics became during the Cold War era. In the 1960s and '70s, those countries with access to sufficient foreign credit adopted a debt-led structure. This approach returned somewhat to commodity exports as a path to development, but trading imbalances and

DOI: 10.4324/9781003283843-5

fiscal shortcomings coupled with the external shocks of the 1970s oil crises led the way to hemispheric labor organization evidenced by **1978 ABC Metalworker's Strike** in Brazil.

Throughout these events, the themes of urbanization, the urban/rural dichotomy, and informality emerge as Latin America shifted from a rural to urban society. By the end of the 1930–1980 period, Latin America was the most urbanized region in the world. While industry was not restricted to urban areas, it was attracted to the more advanced infrastructure and abundant labor force that cities offered. This chapter also underscores the considerable presence of authoritarian regimes, which implemented sweeping state-led initiatives that arguably grew economies and increased development, but at the expense of democratic freedoms as they used terror tactics to retain power.

Stock Market Crash, October 29, 1929 (New York City, United States)

When the United States stock market crashed in 1929 ushering in the Great Depression, the downturn reverberated globally. As the United States and the United Kingdom were key trading partners and investors in the region, the crash also sent shockwaves to Latin America. The ripple effect in the region, however, was less dramatic than it was in the United States. In 1935, the US economy was still reeling, with the national income 25 percent smaller than it had been in 1929.[1] In contrast, Colombia had already recovered to pre-Depression production levels by 1932, and Brazil, Mexico, Argentina, El Salvador, Guatemala, and Chile reached this milestone in 1937. In fact, 16 of the region's 20 countries had recovered by the end of the decade.[2]

Several reasons explain the region's ability to weather this external shock. First, the prices and volume of many of the primary products that Latin America exported had already peaked and were in decline in the late 1920s. This downturn was a marker of the more dramatic turn in the Great Depression, but in Latin America it served to soften the blow. Second, whereas failing banks and lending institutions were a hallmark of the Great Depression in the United States and the developed world, most of Latin America's recently reformed banks had substantial currency reserves and weathered the stormy economy. This was particularly true of the central banks that had formed or were solidified in the wake of World War I. While they suffered under declining export prices, these banks had invested in government bonds, receiving interest payments that kept them afloat until export prices recovered. National decisions to forgo many foreign debt repayments in the wake of the global crisis created a larger cushion. Ultimately, Latin American banks escaped with bumps and bruises, avoiding the faceplanting of many financial institutions in the United States and Western Europe.

The softened impact of the Great Depression, however, did not preclude the crisis from having dramatic effects on the region. On the contrary, it accelerated important structural and economic transitions that saw an increasing role of the state in national economies between 1930 and 1980. These changes included more direct state involvement in economic strategies and greater product and agricultural diversification. Smaller changes also proved significant, such as an introduction of income and land tax systems in light of the reduced import duties and export revenues the Depression brought. This does not mean that the export-led model dominating from 1870 to 1930 was entirely dismissed. On the eve of the Great Depression, in fact, in half of the region's countries, one export made up over 50 percent of exports.[3] That sort of importance does not dissipate overnight, even with a large shock like the Great Depression. In 1939, the industrial share of the economy was still less than 20 percent in every country, except for Argentina.[4] So it should come as no surprise that in most countries, particularly in most smaller countries, exports were one key factor to Latin America's Great Depression recovery.

Government expenditures, investment, and local consumption also helped economies bounce back. As the export sector began to recover, money flowed in, giving Latin Americans purchasing power. As a result, consumers demanded more goods and services. But in a global era of protectionism arising in the post–World War I and Depression era, the imported products they had grown accustomed to were even more expensive. In many larger and Southern Cone countries, governments proactively strove to improve their trade balance. This meant that once economic conditions started to improve, they instituted a combination of tariffs and exchange rate policies that both made national products more attractive than imports to consumers and made exports cheaper and more attractive for foreigners to buy. The collapse of the gold standard by 1933 presented another mechanism by which governments could impact trade: they used a combination of devaluing their currencies, using different exchange rates for different sectors, and raising import tariffs on certain goods to make domestically produced consumer products more attractive to national buyers.[5]

To understand the importance of exchange rates and these trade policies, it is helpful to imagine yourself as a tourist visiting another country. In this country you go out one day to buy some presents for family members back home. When you start to calculate the exchange rate, you realize that the amount you budgeted for presents allows you to buy many more presents produced by local artisans than you had imagined and at a much better price than you could pay at home, so you end up buying more, maybe even saving some for future presents. In this case, you have visited a country where the exchange rate is weak compared to the currency you earn, which has inspired you to spend more money. The same decisions led Latin American consumers to buy Latin American–produced products, as government-introduced exchange rates and tariff policies made domestically produced items more affordable.

The challenge in Latin America was that many intermediate and capital goods, like machines needed to make the finished goods people wanted to buy, still had to be imported. In order to incentivize production at home, governments created multiple exchange rates in different economic sectors. The sectors that benefited the most under these semi-artificial conditions were the industrial manufacturing sectors that were established before World War I. This process, whereby *burgeoning industries are protected from foreign competition by the government until they are mature enough to compete*, is often termed **import substitution industrialization**. During this period of state-led growth, this strategy arguably proved successful in the Southern Cone, in larger countries, and, to a certain extent, in mid-sized countries. Argentina, for example, opened over 15,000 industrial firms between 1935 and 1941 and the value of industrial goods produced between 1935 and 1945 tripled.

Whereas larger, Southern Cone countries and Colombia took a proactive approach to manipulating the exchange rates, most smaller countries in the Caribbean, and Central America, had a reactive response. Currencies in these countries also became devalued, but it was a result of having national currencies pegged at a fixed exchange ratio to the US dollar. This choice arose amidst a long history of US intervention during the export-led growth period that left weakened political and financial systems. For these countries, devaluation was de facto, rather than direct.

The importation of finished goods from the United States accompanied US intervention in customs houses during the export-led period, meaning that these smaller countries lacked pre-war industrial infrastructure. In these countries, most national production diversification occurring in the 1930s and '40s was not so much import substitution industrialization as it was import substitution agriculture. Instead of importing staple food and agricultural products, farmers shifted to produce and sell these products domestically, catering to increasing domestic demand. From cotton for textiles to vegetable oil, corn, and beans, farmers in small countries, just like in large countries, diversified production to adjust for a lack of imports and the increasing population. The countries with the least flexibility to switch agricultural production were those in Central America and the Caribbean with substantial tracts of land controlled by multinational banana and sugar companies, respectively (see the United Fruit Company in Chapter 4). But even countries like Cuba, the Dominican Republic,

El Salvador, and Guatemala experienced some degree of diversification, alongside Depression-era government intervention and banking reforms.

Import substitution industrialization and agriculture did diversify production in Latin America; however, it did little to improve efficiency or increase productivity, the amount each worker produced. Keeping competition at bay disincentivized implementing new technologies and slowed the development of programs to train laborers. Restricted access to credit and electric power needed to sustain advancements also kept productivity low, particularly in the industrial sector. In the United States the average factory employed 43 workers in 1939, but Latin America's most industrialized countries (Argentina, Brazil, Chile, Colombia, Mexico, and Uruguay) lagged considerably.[6] To address this low productivity within a state-led economic model required even more intervention. Populist political leaders, like Lázaro Cárdenas in Mexico, embraced this approach.

In 1938, Lázaro Cárdenas, the president of Mexico, nationalized the oil industry after foreign refineries refused to acquiesce to a collective bargaining agreement that would have established a 40-hour work week for petroleum workers. In a display of populism that combined radio technology and appeals to the growing share of industrial workers, Cárdenas announced the founding of Petroleos Mexicanos (PEMEX), a **nationalization** that *unilaterally transferred all private property of the resource into the hands of the state*. His speech was transmitted live before he even announced the change to his cabinet members. Foreign oil companies with significant investments off Mexico's Gulf Coast, like Royal Dutch Shell and Standard Oil of New Jersey, were caught completely off guard. Ultimately, nationalizing Mexican oil mitigated energy shortages needed to fuel industrial production in Mexico, but it did little to incentivize productivity and efficiency changes.

PEMEX represents a pinnacle of direct state intervention in the 1930s, but state intervention was neither new nor restricted to nationalizations. In the 1920s in the wake of World War I, some municipal, state, and federal governments took over road construction and maintenance, railroads, and energy production. Some of the most impactful interventions during the 1930s in small and larger countries alike were government-driven road expansions. At its best, these roads stimulated backward linkages of concrete production and forward linkages of complex bus systems serving passengers and cargo transport through the twenty-first century. At its worst, these roads further eroded what remained of communal landholding and semi-autonomous Indigenous groups throughout the region and fundamentally altered ecosystems.

The state-led growth model depended on popular support for government intervention into economic sectors throughout the mid-twentieth century. State oversight came through development banks and institutions offering support and credit for new ventures. And government intervention often included worker concessions in the form of minimum wages, pensions, and worker training programs. Workers, at least male workers, were voters. Cárdenas's decision to announce PEMEX via radio was so popular that women, who would not get to vote in Mexico until 1953, began a movement to donate jewelry and cash to help Cárdenas indemnify the expelled oil companies.[7] In 1940s Argentina, Juan Perón's appeal to urban workers garnered him intense loyalty lasting well into the 1970s.[8] Politicians, however, had to toe a difficult line of supporting industrialists in burgeoning sectors who controlled much of the capital, while also appealing to the popular classes, increasingly urban laborers, whose vote determined their success in office. Perhaps the nicknames of Brazil's populist dictator-turned-president, Getúlio Vargas, best sum up these tensions. Known as both the "father of the poor" and the "mother to the rich," the resulting economic policies often reflected the embedded contradictions and the challenges that could result from state-led growth.

One reason that industrial laborers' positions grew more important was the increasing urbanization in Latin America. Industrial jobs were more often available in cities, which also concentrated better educational resources, social services, and facilitated worker organization through union activities and collectives. Declining agricultural export prices in the 1930s also incentivized agricultural laborers to look elsewhere for work. With immigration at a virtual halt in the 1930s, internal migrants became the newest addition to the urban working class. Most higher-paying formal sector jobs were available to men between the ages of 18 and 35, but women, although often excluded from the industrial workforce or restricted to food and textile sectors, also migrated to cities. They often found work in the service sector as domestic workers, selling products in local markets, or working in the informal market. In 1930, just 32 percent of the region's population lived in urban areas, but by 1950, 42 percent lived in cities. The fact that Latin America's population increased from 100 to 158 million in the same period means that over 34 million new inhabitants came to live in these urban areas, many of which had over 20,000 inhabitants (see Figure 5.1). The transition was not always directly into the formal labor market: the share of informal urban workers was consistent throughout the region, representing between 10 and 20 percent of the national working population in 1950.[9]

Thus, on the eve of World War II, even Latin America's most industrialized economies were in a semi-nascent state and facing considerable challenges. Industrial production had increased, but many sectors were still reliant on imported inputs needed to create those products. Furthermore, production was no longer guaranteed and depended on government intervention. Even with an increase in jobs created by direct and indirect

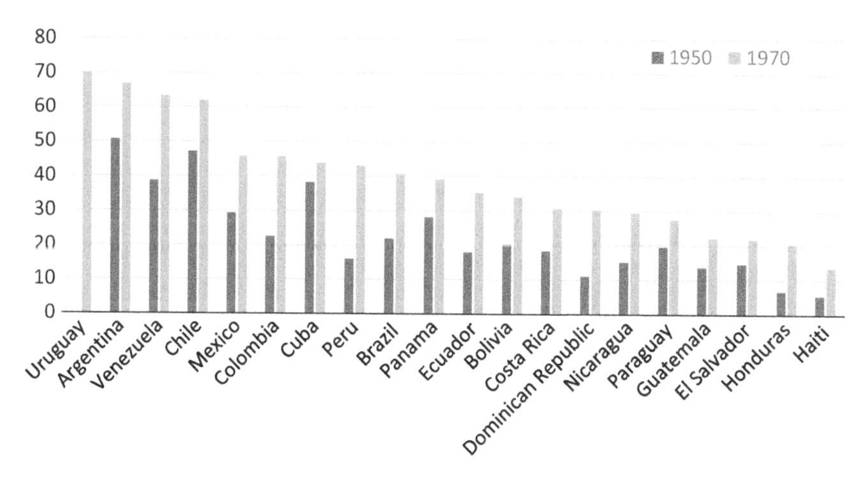

Figure 5.1 Percentage of population living in urban areas of 20,000 or more inhabitants: 1950 and 1970. ECLAC. United Nations. CEPALSTAT. "Database of Demographic Bulletin No. 75: Latin America: Urbanization and Urban Population Trends."

intervention, people struggled to find formal employment and the stability it afforded. City infrastructures were easily overwhelmed by rapid urbanization and inhabitants increasingly demanded not just jobs, but also social services. Their voting power and ability to stall industrial production through strikes and labor organizations influenced politics. In contrast, residents in the countryside, which was over 50 percent of Latin America's population in 1950, struggled to mobilize for better working conditions amidst exploitative labor regimes and large-scale farming.

ECLA founded, 1948 (Santiago, Chile)

Like the Great Depression, World War II served as an external shock to the region with a dramatic impact on economic trajectories. Brazil was the only country to send troops (fighting for the Allies), but the war restricted Latin America's main trading partners' ability to import many commodities and raw materials from the region. In response, the United States coordinated with Latin American leaders to increase US importation of Latin American goods, which absorbed some of the shock from the wartime trade disruption. The volume of Latin American exports remained low, but the value of exports increased. Rising import costs and inflation, however, tempered these export revenue gains. Latin Americans depended on imported capital and finished goods from Western Europe and the United States, but these materials just trickled in, and when they arrived there was not only high demand (due to a lack of supply), but also more currency available to buy products. As foreign money was exchanged for local currency to buy local products due to shortages, retail prices in Latin America for domestic and foreign products increased by over 10 percent.

Waning imports also reduced revenues. The region imposed high customs duties in the 1930s to encourage Latin American industrial production, but the measures did not diminish imports. By the start of the war, these customs duties accounted for up to 50 percent of government income. Direct income taxes were still rare in Latin American at the time, and the loss of customs duties left governments with less to spend on a range of measures, including social services. The dramatic shocks the war brought to the trade and economic sector encouraged Latin American leaders to look inward for a solution, a strategy that at times could challenge post-war global economic tendencies.

In the post-war era, the newly established World Bank and United Nation's International Monetary Fund (IMF) were willing to try and control inflation and to stabilize currencies in their quest to build back war-torn economies. They wanted to strengthen developing economies and prevent another Great Depression and World War II. A number of UN member nations also adopted the **General Agreement on Tariffs and Trade (GATT)**, *a multinational treaty to reduce quotas, subsidies, and tariffs that remained relevant to global trade through 1995*. The IMF, World Bank, and GATT treaty were signs of a general global trend toward reversing the protectionism of the interwar years.

Latin American UN representatives believed that these efforts were not sufficient to address the volatile market prices the region suffered. Since independence, volatile prices and trade imbalances had plagued the region and World War II had exacerbated these imbalances. Latin Americans advocated for additional oversight from the UN, noting that commodity exports were much more susceptible to global price and production fluctuations than finished goods. Essentially, Latin America continued to be highly vulnerable to volatility any time a major global crisis emerged, and many of the region's economists and leaders argued that unless the global trade imbalances impacting production of primary goods like coffee, sugar, and copper were explicitly addressed, the region would continue to struggle economically.

Chile's representative to the United Nations proposed a new group to address region-specific challenges – the Economic Commission for Latin America, ECLA (CEPAL in Spanish and Portuguese and today ECLAC to include the Caribbean). Similar to the Marshall Plan implemented to rebuild European economies, Latin Americans insisted that a regional approach was required to catch up to developed countries. When the proposal came to a vote in the United Nations, despite reservations from the

United States, Canada, and the Soviet Union, the ECLA passed, opening its doors in Santiago, Chile in June 1948.

Raúl Prebisch, an Argentine economist, led the commission in name and in practice for decades. In 1949, Prebisch published a manifesto, one that was quickly translated into Portuguese. In the manifesto, the economist introduced the concept of core and periphery that was the closest to an ECLA ideology that came to exist. For Prebisch the step-by-step development espoused by W.W. Rostow and many North American and European scholars failed to acknowledge unequal trading dynamics between center and peripheral nations.[10] Center nations bought primary goods from peripheral nations while peripheral nations largely imported manufactured goods from center nations. The trade imbalance lay in the fact that primary product prices declined more than manufactured prices, creating a structural gap between country groups. As long as Latin America was producing these primary products, they would always be behind. The ECLA structuralists, more commonly referred to as **dependistas**, were convinced that *creating export markets for goods beyond commodities was essential for peripheral countries to make the transition to become developed countries*. These ECLA structuralists served as a counterpoint for economists who largely followed the University of Chicago economic model that emphasized financial management. Known as **monetarists**, they *advocated for curbing excessive monetary expansion and exchange rate mismanagement and moving toward credit stability*. For monetarists, *low inflation and monetary stability were the keys to development*.

In Chile, the ECLA found a flourishing intellectual environment where economists, sociologists, and other social scientists debated the nuances of the inward-development approach.[11] Their impact quickly spread well beyond theoretical debates. Offices opened in Mexico City and Rio de Janeiro in 1951, and politicians and policy experts, desperate to appeal to voters who felt the brunt of economic volatility brought on by World War II, implemented initiatives to adhere to ECLA directives. During the period of state-led growth, the ECLA had the greatest direct impact on the economies of Chile and Brazil.[12]

The Great Depression and wartime experiences provided some insight into possible strategies to encourage this transition toward the ECLA inward-looking model. Direct involvement from the state, for example, could jumpstart industrial production. During the 1930s and World War II, Latin American governments' willingness to incentivize nontradable production, goods made in the country for domestic consumption, injected life into industrial sectors and to national economies. Many of these policies, however, had been implemented in an ad hoc manner. The ECLA espoused a deliberate approach to stimulate production. The approach included increasing regional trading and lessening the dependence on US and Western European trading partners to spur a transition toward producing intermediate and capital goods in the entire region. So, while the IMF continued to encourage Latin American development using an outward growth approach, ECLA adherents concertedly turned their focus inward.

Countries that had already seen a fair degree of industrialization during the 1920s and '30s – Argentina, Brazil, Chile, Colombia, Mexico, and Uruguay – placed manufacturing at the center of the development plan. Drawing on post–Great Depression experiences, they increased tariffs and implemented import quotas (in the case of Mexico and Uruguay) to artificially protect nascent manufacturing from competing imports. The impact on consumers was substantial. In Chile, the average tariff on a nondurable good, like a T-shirt or a pair of shoes, reached 328 percent in 1960. The rate in the European Economic Community averaged just 17 percent. Tariff trade costs are often passed onto consumers, meaning Chileans could pay about 20 times more for a T-shirt imported from the United States than Europeans did for the same item. This trend countered a global move toward lower tariffs ushered in with the GATT, putting many Latin American countries at odds with many developed countries' trade policies.

Diversification strategies proved somewhat successful in the Southern Cone and in the large countries of Brazil and Mexico. Domestic demand slowly shifted away from imported finished goods, which could include anything from clothing and appliances to films. It is within this context of government protections that Mexico's Golden Age of Cinema emerged, the era in which the Spanish filmmaker Luis Buñuel directed films like *Los Olvidados*, which opens this book. Brazilian and Argentine governments also helped develop film industries that could compete with Hollywood. Smaller countries simply did not have the populations to support such diversification initiatives.[13]

Small- and some medium-sized countries in the region may not have had a manufacturing head start, but they too saw industrialization as a goal. Import-substituted agriculture had been relatively successful in the 1930s, but the idea of creating regional integration programs to incentivize industrial production gained popularity under the ECLA. In 1951, El Salvador, Guatemala, Nicaragua, and Costa Rica formed the Central American Common Market, and in 1969, the Andean Group united Colombia, Peru, and Venezuela. By facilitating trade within these blocs, countries could come to specialize in some, rather than all, industrial sectors. The blocs would also increase the size of the potential consumer market. Thus, regional integration could make the import substitution industrialization achieved in larger economies accessible to smaller countries. The effectiveness of these regional programs was lackluster in the period of state-led growth, but important infrastructure was established and utilized in the era of market-driven changes from the 1980s forward (see NAFTA in Chapter 6).

The successes of state-led growth through high protection often backfired for consumers. Many items were more expensive or simply unavailable. As a silver lining, department stores began to offer installment payment plans. By allowing customers to pay smaller increments over the course of multiple months rather than in one lump sum, some lower- and middle-income buyers received their first access to credit. The installments also became a distinctive Latin American shopping feature, and today buyers can use installment plans to buy items and services ranging from cell phones and clothing to vacation packages and hotel stays. High protection also left producers severely constrained, as they imported equipment and intermediate goods needed to successfully make this transition.

An additional challenge was that domestic investment could not adequately support the expensive nature of growing manufacturing industries. To recalibrate, Latin American nations once again looked abroad, seeing multinational corporations' capital as critical to success in these burgeoning sectors. This reversal from the 1930s, which saw the nationalization of oil, banking, and transportation sectors, allowed for foreign companies to develop products in a captive market. And the market was growing: Latin America's population more than doubled between 1950 and 1980. With high tariff rates keeping foreign competitors out, multinational companies ranging from Ford, General Motors, and Volkswagen to General Electric, Coca-Cola, and Nestlé could profit off increasing Latin American demand with minimal competition. These multinationals also benefited from the multiple exchange rates that developed to address the intermediate and capital good shortages. For multinational executives, dealing with these "geologic" layers of protection could be dizzying, but the profits were enticing. As many of these multinationals were headquartered in the United States, Latin America's welcoming of multinational companies further complexified hemispheric geopolitical dynamics.

The ECLA was not solely focused on foreign trade. Adherents also looked to transform structural challenges within Latin America. For example, they zeroed in on landholding inequities that plagued the region since the colonial period, but which had concentrated in the nineteenth century and export-led growth periods. To take a systematic approach to these problems entailed collecting data on the economic and social situation in the region. One of the ECLA's first tasks was requesting complete statistical records and data from countries on everything from trade to wage data. Since independence, such records had been collected sporadically, but rarely for a sustained period and in a unifying way across the region or even a single country. Many decennial censuses were unreliable or incomplete, and consistent information on wages, prices, exchange rates, and rents were nearly impossible to find. Literacy rates, for example, could refer to everyone above the age of 5 in one country and everyone above the age of 15 in another. It is due to the ECLA's mission to gather these data, a mission that continues through today, that our historical understanding of the region's economic history becomes more nuanced starting in the second half of the twentieth century.

Once these data were collected, wealth distribution and urban/rural and sectoral divergences became even more apparent. Within the region, large- and medium-sized countries had narrowed the gap to Southern Cone countries in a number of indicators, from production and GDP per capita to schooling and literacy rates, but smaller countries lagged woefully behind. One reason was that rural agriculture still dominated in these areas. Many *campesinos*, landless agricultural workers, were contracted to work on large plantations or *latifundios* connected to the commodity export market. In these areas, schools were rare and underfunded; the prospects of owning land, let alone getting into the export market, were virtually nonexistent; and exploitative labor practices persisted. To improve their quality of life often required *campesinos* to move to a city where there were better educational and health services. This is what many did. Even after moving, however, these new migrants provided a relatively inelastic labor supply, meaning that even when wages declined considerably, industrialists could easily find people willing to fill vacant positions. Under these conditions, production increased overall, but there were few efficiency gains in the amount of productivity per worker.

By the 1960s, deficiencies of the inward-looking and state-led development model were apparent, but amidst complex tariffs and growing bureaucracies, state-led growth persisted. And it did so on both sides of the political ideological spectrum: ECLA members served as advisors to Fidel Castro in communist Cuba and worked alongside the United States' Alliance for Progress, a coalition that attempted to curb communism in the region. Large governments set their sights on expanding industrial production by promoting industrial exports. To do so, however, required another layer of protection, one that would incentivize domestic producers to export their products rather than sell them at home. Between 1965 and 1980, the number of **state-owned enterprises (SOEs)** increased substantially. These ventures, *in which the government controlled commercial interests in a variety of sectors from public services to energy and mining*, had been increasing in number since the state-led growth period and *operated from the national to the local level*. Now they expanded well beyond transportation, communication, and electricity. Although many of these new SOEs only operated profitably because of substantial investments and protectionist measures, Brazil's Empresa Brasileira de Aeronáutica (Embraer) is an example of the success that could be achieved. Today

Embraer is a leading supplier of commercial aircraft, but when it became an SOE in 1969, its charge was to make planes for Brazil's military.[14]

Twenty-three years after the ECLA was founded, dependista ideas had successfully permeated the region and beyond. Uruguayan intellectual Eduardo Galeano was a key figure in reaching such a broad audience. He made elements of the ECLA structuralist model accessible by distilling complex and debated theories into engaging prose in his 1971 *Open Veins of Latin America*. Galeano, 18 years old when he wrote the book, was a "non-specialized writer [who] wanted to tell a non-specialized public about certain facts that official history, history as told by conquerors, hides or lies about."[15] Galeano himself critiqued the book's oversimplification in 2014, but its initial and continued popularity ensured the dependista legacy for generations in and outside of Latin America, long after the luster of the inward-looking model became tarnished.[16]

Cuban Revolution, 1959 (Havana, Cuba)

On the eve of Cuba's 1959 Revolution, sugar represented 80 percent of Cuba's exports and 54 percent of the country's national income. Even though the US had imposed measures to protect its sugar beet crop in the 1920s, most Cuban sugar exports still went to the United States.[17] The relationship did not stop at sugar, as US companies were heavily involved in multiple sectors, from tourism and public utilities to oil refining and mining. Cuba's economic and political structure meant wealthy landowners, foreign businessmen, and corrupt politicians held considerable sway, while many Cubans remained illiterate and labored tirelessly in agriculture or struggled to make ends meet in growing urban centers. *The Godfather, Part II* provides an accessible, albeit fictional display of the corruption. In the film, Miami mob bosses with connections to Cuban President Fulgencio Batista are profiting from Cuba's casino and underground world, and the godfather, Michael Corleone, is negotiating to expand his operation to Cuba. His pursuits are cut short by the Revolution, which triumphantly takes Havana and forces Batista to flee the island with his family on January 1, 1959, a scene captured in the movie. By 1961, all production passed into state control. Cuba's state-led socialism nationalized all sectors, including farms and mining, as well as hotels and casinos entangled with the mob. The movie never returns to Cuba, but the Revolution served as a watershed in modern Latin American economic history. Within the context of the Cold War, it brought a communist nation within 100 miles of the United States. The Revolution also reflected the broad criticism throughout the region related to its development inequalities.

The Revolution was led by Fidel Castro, a Cuban law student whose political career had once been thwarted by canceled elections, and Ernesto Che Guevara, an Argentine doctor who had been radicalized on a 1948 motorcycle trek through South America to study leprosy. Together they galvanized disparate groups, including disenfranchised and marginalized rural laborers, under the 26th of July movement. Castro, Guevara, and their followers believed a meaningful revolution could start with the rural peasantry just as much as the urban proletariat. Communism, however, was not a definitive goal when the movement started in 1956. Guevara followed Leninist ideology and was committed to radical economic and social change, but Castro was not as clear on the best direction for Cuba. He was committed to diversifying Cuba's trade partners to diminish the de facto economic sway the United States held over the island.

In May 1960, Cuba asked US oil companies to refine crude Soviet oil. Embroiled in the Cold War, US companies refused, so Cuba responded by expropriating Texaco, Standard Oil, and Shell, taking over control of operations without compensation to the companies. Tensions escalated quickly between the two countries. When the United States completely cut off sugar imports from Cuba, Cuba expropriated US properties, including prosperous agricultural latifundios and companies like Sears and Coca-Cola. After the failed Bay of Pigs military invasion on Playa Girón, Castro forged an allegiance with the Soviets. In 1962, aerial surveillance revealed Soviet nuclear warhead shells en route to the small Caribbean nation. The Cuban missile crisis ensued, representing the height of nuclear tensions between the two superpowers. While the US President Kennedy and the Soviet Union First Secretary Kruschev reached a compromise which averted nuclear war, the impact in Latin America marked a "before and after" moment, further entangling economics and hemispheric politics.[18] The fall of the Soviet Union in 1991 necessitated Cuba restructuring the economy in the 1990s, but the extent of the economic relationship between the United States and Cuba was largely restricted to remittances and items sent to the island from exiles or family members until Castro stepped down as de facto dictator in 2008.[19]

Cubans did not always agree with the communist direction that the Revolution took, but many had joined the movement in the 1950s ready for change. Rural sugar laborers had faced more extreme challenges since the 1920s. Amidst protectionist measures from their largest trading partner, the United States, sugar producers struggled to increase profits. Owners of the *large landed estates connected to the export market*, ***latifundios***, *that depended on low wage and debt peonage laborers* cut costs by decreasing the harvest period. This left greater underemployment and poverty. Many insurgents called for structural change that would address persistent social and economic inequities. In the 1950s, the top 10 percent of Cuban wealth owners controlled 40 percent of wealth and the top 20 percent controlled 60 percent. Meanwhile Cuba's poorest 20 percent, a disproportionate share of whom were Afro-Cubans, controlled just over 2 percent of

Cuba's wealth. Land inequality, which had increased in the nineteenth century and export-led growth period, was even starker. Large latifundios and *minifundios*, subsistence land holdings, served as the two dominant land structures on opposite ends of the spectrum. Outside of the agricultural sector, the urban middle class was increasingly disgruntled with the Batista dictatorship's corruption, adding another layer of dissent. The urban poor and working class also struggled. Many Cubans like María de los Reyes Castillo Bueno felt "there was terrible poverty; the unsanitary conditions in the poor neighbourhoods were alarming; many children didn't go to school; there was no work and no social security whatsoever," in addition to pervasive state violence.[20] As a mother, she supported the 26th of July movement by covering for her sons, who were involved.

Cubans' dissatisfaction with the status quo reflected sentiments resonating throughout Latin America, where persistently high income and land inequality disadvantaged the region's poorest populations. The state-led model was leading to economic growth (particularly in large- and mid-sized countries), but for the most part, political, business, and agricultural elites continued to disproportionately benefit: Latin America's poorest 20 percent controlled just 3.7 percent of the region's wealth in 1960.[21] The ECLA, concerned not only with global commodity imbalances, but also with domestic restructuring, turned to land reform as a mechanism to try and address these inequities.[22] They hoped that more equitable land distribution through mid-sized farms, rather than large latifundios and miniscule minifundios, would lead to more efficient agriculture and would increase the poorer population's incomes to the point that they would demand and consume locally produced industrial goods.

It should come as no surprise that Cuba was neither the first nor last country to institute land reform. As early as the 1930s Mexico redistributed 45 million acres of uncultivated, arable land to 12,000 villages.[23] In Guatemala, a 1944 democratic revolution opened the door to land reform in the small country where just 2 percent of the population had controlled 74 percent of the arable land. When Guatemala expanded land reform to redistribute arable but undeveloped land to 100,000 peasant families, the United Fruit Company (UFC, see Chapter 4) found itself particularly impacted as only 15 percent of UFC land was cultivated. In Bolivia, just 6 percent of landowners held 90 percent of cultivated land. Here the National Revolutionary Movement espoused splitting up large agricultural estates to provide credits and technical assistance to smaller landholders. While these land reforms were substantial, none effectively restructured the system. Mexico's reform only reached half the campesino population and 57 percent of land was left in the hands of large landowners. Guatemalan reforms were reversed in subsequent years after their president was ousted, a move heralded by the UFC; and in Bolivia, only 18 percent of land was redistributed, benefiting just 39 percent of campesinos. Land reform efforts in 1960s Chile and Peru were similarly lackluster, reaching less than one-third of the campesino population.[24] In Cuba, the radicalized revolution did shift the balance. By 1970, Cuba's poorest 20 percent controlled almost 8 percent of wealth. The share that the richest 20 percent controlled dropped to 35 percent from the 60 percent it had controlled just a decade before. While the mid-sized farms that the ECLA had hoped for failed to materialize under Castro's agrarian reform, the restructuring did make a dent in persistent inequality.

Cuba's expropriation of refineries and production also built on earlier trends. Nationalizations were relatively common during this period, particularly in sectors that concerned natural resources and infrastructure. When Cárdenas created PEMEX in 1938, he followed a similar nationalization as Bolivia had enacted in 1937. As early as the 1920s, some countries wrought control of trains and transportation systems, which had often been owned by foreigners or multinational corporations. Cuba's Revolution, however, created a space where Latin American calls for land reform and expropriations could easily be conflated with communism.

In an effort to prevent similar revolutions, the United States initiated a hemispheric Alliance for Progress in 1961. Its goal was to improve Latin America's economy, and its policies and initiatives often embraced the ECLA structuralists' calls for development funding, credit, and land reform. Billions of dollars poured into Latin America. One of the chief recipients of Alliance for Progress funding was Chile.[25] As such, when voters democratically elected the socialist Salvador Allende as their president in 1970, Chile was seen as an Alliance for Progress failure. Allende expanded land reform initiated in the 1960s and expropriated Chilean copper mines. In return, Chile was mischaracterized as another Cuba, and the country faced an immediate reduction in international economic aid and loans, further complicating a rocky economic reality of inflation, shortages, and instability. The economic chaos created popular support for a coup among many Chileans, including urban middle-class women who had supported Allende's candidacy in 1970. Consequently, he was ousted in a military coup on September 11, 1973. Under General Augusto Pinochet's subsequent dictatorship (1973–1989), thousands of Chileans were disappeared or tortured.[26] Pinochet's anti-communist stance encouraged international loans to return, despite the persistent state terror tactics keeping him in power through 1989.

Human rights abuses abounded not only in Pinochet's Chile, but in regimes throughout the region during the state-led period. In the Dominican Republic, Rafael Trujillo's ultra-nationalistic dictatorship (1939–1961) terrorized residents, particularly Haitian descendants. Trujillo expanded the state bureaucracy and public employees, even actively courting hotel employees, barbers, and domestic works to inform on dissidents. He went so far as to offer combs and chairs, and even opened a barber shop in the small city of Neyba in exchange for intelligence gathering.[27] Military dictatorships in the Southern Cone in the 1960s and '70s imposed censorship and terror and strengthened propaganda to keep dissent at bay. Even in Castro's Cuba, dissenters of communism or those seen as a threat were sent to labor camps, where they toiled on sugar plantations under inhumane conditions.

Authoritarian regimes could more easily implement significant reforms, and GDP per capita and productivity grew substantially between 1945 and 1973. Those that embraced anti-communism received international aid and loans, facilitating state projects, from dams and highways to schools and medical centers. By the 1960s, many even turned away from a purely industrialized growth plan and espoused diversifying export agriculture by introducing new export commodities like soy and tropical fruits. This period is often termed the "golden age" of Latin American economic growth. Growth and productivity improved regionally, but the large economies fared the best. Brazil and Mexico experienced annual GDP per capita growth rates of 4.1 percent and 3.4 percent, respectively, equaling and surpassing rates in industrialized Europe (3.5 percent) and the United States (2.2 percent) during the same time period.[28] In terms of growth, which was increasingly a combination of state-led and debt-led growth, Latin America was starting to catch up to the developed world. The increased entry of women into the labor market explains some of this growth, but not all: there were clear efficiency gains during this state-led period. Development indicators, like education rates and mortality, also improved.

At the start of the state-led period in 1930, not even half of Latin American adults were literate. In the subsequent 50 years, education expanded substantially. In the 1950s, "important gains in access to education at all levels resulted from this convergence of social, political, and economic forces."[29] Education programs in Peru, for example, targeted adult campesinos and the discussion and provision of bilingual education surfaced in countries with large Indigenous populations. Castro's Literacy Campaign in 1961 mobilized Cuba's literate population to educate the country's illiterate adult population.[30] The success was remarkable, as boys and girls as young as 12 years old went into neighborhoods and rural areas, effectively halving Cuba's illiteracy rate, making it the lowest in Latin America and close to rates in the United States and Western Europe. Migration toward cities also helped to improve literacy and schooling rates as educational resources were easier to access. Education continued to be a priority across the region as more authoritarian governments came to power in the 1960s and '70s. Curricula, however, shifted away from topics of citizenship and democracy and toward skills-based materials. And at the university level, professors, departments, and students critical of authoritarian regimes became targets of state violence or were forced to become exiles. Nevertheless, by 1980, eight of ten adults could read, an over 30 percent improvement from the start of the state-led period.[31] These development gains, as well as the continued economic growth, partially explain the persistence of authoritarian regimes in the region.

Despite substantial literacy gains between 1930 and 1980, Latin America as a region remained behind Western Europe and the United States. Guatemala, Honduras, Nicaragua, and Haiti still had literacy rates below 70 percent. Only Argentina, Uruguay, Costa Rica, and Cuba had rates above 90 percent. Literacy also did not necessarily equate to adequate schooling. Investments in university-level education disproportionately benefited privileged groups, and in 1960 the bulk of Latin America's working population still had no formal schooling. By 1980 this was still the case in Guatemala and Haiti, but the maximum education that most Latin Americans could hope for was still abysmal: one to three years in Colombia, Honduras, Panama, Paraguay, and Peru, and four to six years in Argentina, Brazil, Costa Rica, Cuba, Ecuador, Uruguay, and Venezuela. Only in Chile was there substantially more schooling, with one-third of the economically active population completing the equivalent of some high school.[32] By comparison, 80 percent of US workers had completed a high school education in 1981.[33] These educational deficiencies kept Latin America underdeveloped: as long as only a handful of Latin Americans were receiving the highest training, wage differentials between skilled and unskilled workers would remain high, continuing the tradition of persistent income inequality.

One challenge to providing adequate education was a growing school-age population. Outside of the Southern Cone, the region's population grew 2.7 percent annually between 1950 and 1980 as mortality and life expectancy rates improved. In 1930, the typical Latin American could expect to live until the age of 34. By 1950, life expectancy had risen to over 50 in many countries and was as high as 66 in Uruguay. By 1980, regional life expectancy had nearly doubled, reaching 64 years of age, and several countries enjoyed life expectancies over 70. Even in countries where the 1980 life expectancies had not yet reached 60, they had improved by 10–15 years between 1950 and 1980.[34] As fertility rates remained high during the period, only starting to decline noticeably in the 1970s, a demographic bulge of children emerged. Thus, childrearing and responsibilities continued to keep many women out of the formal labor market during the state-led period. It was only in the 1970s that women of prime child-bearing age (20–35) became more actively involved in the formal labor force, and their employment was often in the service sector. This sector did not benefit from export protections or state-led initiatives, meaning women's entry into the labor force did little to address regional gender inequalities.[35] In countries where fertility rates exceeded five children per woman, female participation in the formal labor market remained low. This does not mean, however, that women did not work. In urban areas, for example, they could often find informal or piece-rate work to supplement household income. The one exception was Haiti, where agriculture remained the main sector of employment. Here, despite fertility rates of 5.4 and life expectancy of just 53 years, two-thirds of women worked, with most working in agriculture.[36]

Concurrent with population growth was the incredible urbanization rate. By 1950, Latin America's urban share had grown to 42 percent. The urbanization rate then rose 4.4 percent annually between 1950 and 1970, a rate unprecedented worldwide. By 1980, 65 percent of the region's population lived in cities, and Latin America was the most urbanized region of the world. The non-agricultural share of the workforce shifted accordingly. Whereas in 1950, one-third of the working-age population was still employed in traditional agriculture, by 1980, that share had dropped to just 19 percent. Only in Central America and Haiti did most of the population remain outside of cities. As many educational and standards-of-living gains came from the move to urban areas, development indicators in these countries lagged behind the region as a whole. Under authoritarian governments, some infrastructure, telecommunications, and public utilities in remote rural areas helped to alleviate urban/rural disparities during the period of state-led growth. The legacy of these initiatives, however, has been particularly criticized by environmentalists and Indigenous rights advocates, as these measures often expanded export agriculture and further impinged on remaining Indigenous cultural practices and land rights.

Urbanization transferred underemployment from the rural to urban environment. In cities, the accompanying challenges and poverty were more difficult to ignore. Informal housing and commerce were viable solutions for urban and peripheral dwellers. Since the liberal reforms of the mid-nineteenth century, governments had attempted to regulate the housing and commercial activities. Regulations spanned from housing to street vending and peddling codes, but an inability to keep pace with urbanization and to effectively shift cultural practices or to control entrepreneurial endeavors meant that unauthorized housing construction, vending, and transportation persisted, leading to increased informality. By 1980, as much as 20 percent of Latin America's workforce was employed in the urban informal markets, and in Mexico the share reached 44 percent. From *bohíos* in Cuba to *favelas* in Brazil and *poblaciónes callampas* in Chile, informal peripheral housing mushroomed in the urban peripheries.

Despite improved literacy and life expectancy achieved between 1950 and 1970, discontent with the status quo and challenges of unequal development remained. A quick survey of Latin American artistic and religious trends during the state-led period demonstrates how daily economic challenges and realities influenced cultural production. Artists in Cuba's *nueva trova*, the region's *nueva canción*, and Brazil's *música popular brasileira* (MPB) often articulated discontent with political and socio-economic injustice. Victor Jara's 1969 song "Questions for Puerto Montt" serves as a prime example. As he critiques the government's deadly invasion of the shantytown, he eulogizes the victim: "He died without knowing why / they riddled his chest / fighting for the right / to have a floor of his own." New Latin American Cinema like Brazil's *Cinema Novo* and Argentina's Third Cinema also highlighted stark realities.[37] Within the Catholic Church, a faction of priests led a growing social movement of liberation theology that actively promoted social justice and the eradication of misery. Even in countries where authoritarian and anti-communist political regimes took political control in the latter state-led growth period, many artists and church officials continued to critique the status quo, albeit with veiled lyrics and the threat of being disappeared.

ABC Strike, 1978 (São Paulo, Brazil)

In 1978, metalworkers in the metropolitan region of São Paulo, Brazil went on strike. Much industrial production occurred just south of the city proper in three contiguous cities: Santo André, São Bernardo do Campo and São Caetano do Sul. Given the letters of the cities' names, the movement became known as the ABC strike. The value of workers' wages had dropped by as much as 20 percent and they were willing to mobilize during Brazil's military dictatorship. The real wage decline was the culmination of economic policies aimed at stabilizing Brazil's economy in the midst of a fragile global market, and one with drastic implications for Brazil's popular classes. The metalworkers' strike halted production in South America's most industrialized metropolitan area. Led by Luiz Inácio Lula da Silva, known more commonly as Lula, the metalworkers' strike ushered in a period of increasing mobilization in the country.[38] Courts found the strikes illegal and Lula himself ended up imprisoned for a month, but discontent did not disappear. Over one million workers, from schoolteachers to hospital workers, participated in more than 100 strikes in 1979 alone.

The discontent was echoed throughout the region, as worker mobilization increased in the late 1970s. As the state-led growth model transformed, it increasingly became a debt-led growth model, making the region more susceptible to large global fluctuations and external market shocks. Coupled with growing inflationary tendencies of the state-led model, the daily challenges for the status quo proved too much by 1978. In mid- and large-sized countries, many authoritarian regimes were challenged, and in Central America, urban and rural discontent finally coalesced into definable movements.

How did this change take place? If you walk down a US grocery store produce aisle in December, you will discover a clue. Chances are you will find no shortage of fruit, and if you end up buying grapes or kiwis, there is a high probability that your fruit was grown and harvested in Chile. If you head to the refrigerated aisle and pick up some orange juice, there's a good chance that at least some of the oranges were grown in Brazil. This expansion of export agriculture beyond traditional commodity exports like coffee and sugar expanded during the state-led period of growth in the 1960s and 1970s. Despite extraordinary efforts in the region to export manufactured goods globally, the reality was that commodity exports remained the core of Latin America's exports. This was true in countries of all sizes, so Latin America, a land- and natural resource–rich region, revisited the role these sectors could and should play in development.

In the agricultural realm, technology was important in that *modified seeds, pesticides, updated machinery, and expanded irrigation systems*, all part of the **green revolution**, allowed for increased yields and expanded production. The state supported diversifying agricultural exports with development banks, agricultural research institutes, and infrastructure projects such as dams and roads that opened new lands for production. Expansion, however, did not effectively address the minifundio/latifundio dichotomy. Large farms that could produce at scale with modern machinery did not offer increased employment opportunities and small farmers and *campesinos* often moved either into rural peripheries or to cities. Nevertheless, Chile became a fruit, vegetable, and wine exporter; Argentina exported lemons and expanded wheat production using high-yield wheat; Paraguay began planting cotton and soy; and Brazil began exporting soy and oranges. Brazil also focused on improving sugar production, an attempt they hoped would stimulate the country's northeastern economy, which lagged behind the southeast considerably.

Brazil even connected sugar to energy production. Since World War I, scientists and agriculturalists had experimented with using sugarcane bagasse to produce ethanol. In the 1970s, with substantial state investment, they created a viable ethanol energy sector and spurred forward linkages, such as the design of flex fuel engines that could run on both gas and ethanol. The interest in commodity energy production was not restricted to Brazil. After all, energy was one of the key inputs of industrial production not only in Latin America but also globally. Among the oil-rich countries of Mexico, Venezuela, and Ecuador, Mexico had already nationalized oil in 1938, but Venezuela and Ecuador followed suit in 1975 and 1976, respectively. Bolivia invested heavily in natural gas, nationalizing production in 1969, and across the region state investment in dam construction harnessed the power of Latin America's rivers for hydroelectric power. The Itaipu Dam, on the border of Paraguay and Brazil, was a bilateral endeavor that became known as one of the eight engineering wonders of the world.

Expanding agricultural and industrial production and exports was also dependent upon outside funding. Luckily for Latin American politicians and technocrats, these expansions occurred alongside not only an increase in commodity prices, but also a global increase in direct foreign investment. External banks like Citicorp, Santander, and Banco Bilbao began seeking new borrowers around 1966, an effort that increased by 1970. Latin Americans were looking for capital to fund this new level of state-led growth and the growing number of SOEs. Earlier ventures often depended on central banks and international lending organizations like the IMF or the Inter-American Development Bank (IADB), but domestic investment was limited and the IMF and IADB loans came with stipulations set by monetarists. Large- and mid-sized countries heavily capitalized on the era of direct foreign investment: bank lending was just 10 percent of external debt in 1966 but had already jumped up to 26 percent in 1972. Between 1965 and 1980, Latin America received an extraordinary 70 percent of foreign direct investment to the developing world.

There were several important features of these loans that help to explain the crisis that sent workers to the picket line by the end of the 1970s. First, these private bank loans spread the risk among many groups in the hopes of decreasing the chance of defaults. As up to 60 percent of loans could be designated for "general purpose" rather than a specific use, banks did not necessarily know where the money was being invested.[39] Much went to SOEs that might not be profitable otherwise. The other key feature of the loans that made them attractive to lenders was that they had **flexible interest rates**, meaning that their *interest rates would increase or decrease depending on the lending nation's economy*. For most of the 1970s, interest rates remained low while commodity prices were high, a boon to Latin America's mid- and large-sized economies.

Below the surface, this combination of state- and debt-led growth that characterized the 1970s left Latin America in a precarious position. If commodity prices fell (something that historically was bound to happen) and interest rates increased, the region would face significant fiscal challenges. This indeed is what happened in 1978, when the second global oil crisis sent the economies of those foreign lending institutions into a recession, leading them to raise interest rates.[40] The luster of economic growth quickly vanished and the inflation that had been festering expanded. In urbanized countries and those with an export mining sector, worker movements proved destabilizing. In Central America, Nicaragua, El Salvador, and Guatemala, urban workers and *campesinos* formed coalitions, advocating for radical social, political, and economic change. The resulting violence between factions plunged much of Central America into a hotbed of violence and bloodshed in the subsequent decade. This upheaval not only decimated rural and Indigenous populations, but it also incentivized migration and crippled economies.

In Nicaragua, the Somoza regime had been in power since US marines had left the country in 1936. Under the regime one single family controlled the presidency for more than 40 years. More problematic was that same family controlled 60 percent of the nation's economy. In the 1960s, university students, labor unions, and peasant collectives started to organize against the Somozas, naming their movement after a 1930s revolutionary, César Augusto Sandino. In 1979, the Sandinista Revolution took the city of Managua, calling for land reform, unionization, and a mixed economic system that would combine some market-driven characteristics and other socialist elements. Inspired by Cuba, Sandinistas mobilized teenagers in a Literacy Campaign that reduced the country's illiteracy to just 12 percent. For the United States, the Sandinista Revolution was seen as another Cold War failure. In El Salvador, a similar struggle emerged, but here, the right-wing military held the upper hand. In neighboring Guatemala, land reforms had been revoked following a military coup in 1954, and state violence persisted, with Indigenous communities disproportionately suffering. While mid-sized farms in Costa Rica and a thriving banking sector in Panama kept these countries relatively stable, the deterioration of the state-led approach in the 1960s and '70s, coupled with increasing pressure to migrate from agricultural areas, moved many Central Americans toward revolutionary battles.

Elsewhere, inflation proved destabilizing. As foreign direct investment and inflation rose worldwide in the 1970s, so did inflation in the region. For the most part, Latin America's inflation rates kept with world averages, but in the Southern Cone and Brazil, inflation reached triple digits. The structuralists and many ECLA adherents had once seen inflation as a tool to incentivize industrialization and, thus, development. The more advanced Latin American economies had reduced export revenues by encouraging domestic consumption, but at the same time continued to import intermediate and finished goods from abroad. This created a trade imbalance: Latin American countries needed more foreign currency to buy the products they wanted, while foreign demand for Latin American currencies declined (they were not exporting as much). But exchange rates, even when there were multiple exchange rates, were fixed, meaning that currencies became overvalued, particularly in the Southern Cone and Brazil. The resulting inflation became incredibly destabilizing by the end of the decade.

In this environment, currencies were devalued, further increasing incentives to export. The devaluation, however, led to a decrease in real wages and a substantial cost-of-living increase for the working class. Where there were large, industrial workforces, such as the Southern Cone and Brazil, labor pressure incentivized governments to again raise export taxes. The cycle repeated, with inflation and expectations of inflation increasing simultaneously. Although pressure was much stronger in urban centers, workers connected to any export sector felt these impacts. Wives of Bolivian miners, for example, began mobilizing in search of better conditions in the 1960s. Facing criticism from male patriarchy and threats of deportation and arrest, the Housewives Committee of Siglo XX's hunger strikes successfully moved the government to provide concessions to miners and their families.[41]

To address the escalating inflation issue, countries implemented crawling pegs. The hope was that a series of smaller devaluations would be able to stabilize currencies while preventing the shock of a massive devaluation. São Paulo's metalworkers felt otherwise. The ABC metalworkers' strike, then, can be understood as reflective of a culmination of worker and popular-class grievances during the era of inward-looking and state-led growth. The economic growth failed to implement sufficient structural change to address wealth concentration and societal inequities in Latin America. By the end of the 1970s the model also left countries with billions of dollars in foreign loans and crippling interest payments.

Notes

1 Thorp in *Latin America in the 1930s*, p. 8.
2 Honduras, Nicaragua, Cuba, and Uruguay came to recover during or after World War II.
3 See Bulmer-Thomas, *Economic History of Latin America*, 3rd edition, pp. 210–11 for an overview of products.
4 Bulmer-Thomas, *Economic History of Latin America*, 3rd edition, p. 243.
5 Prior to 1929, many larger and Southern Cone countries saw the writing on the wall that the gold standard would go by the wayside. By 1931, Great Britain left and by 1933, the United States.
6 US figure from the United States Bureau of the Census. Historical statistics of the United States, 1789–1945: A supplement to the Statistical abstract of the United States, Volume 789, no. 945. US Government Printing Office, 1949, chapter J. Available https://www2.census.gov/library/publications/1949/compendia/hist_stats_1789-1945/hist_stats_1789-1945-chJ.pdf. Accessed January 22, 2024. Latin America statistics from Bulmer-Thomas, *Economic History of Latin America*, 3rd edition, p. 243. Colombia fared the best with 32 workers per establishment, with Chile (25), Brazil (20), Mexico (20), Argentina (13), and Uruguay (7) trailing behind.
7 See Julieta Sanguino, "La expropiación petrolera de México, el hito que marcó el Gobierno de Lázaro Cárdenas," *El País*, March 18, 2023. https://elpais.com/

mexico/2023-03-18/la-expropiacion-petrolera-de-mexico-el-hito-que-marco-el-gobierno-de-lazaro-cardenas.html.

8 Perón's early appeal also depended considerably on the popular appeal of his first wife, Eva Perón, more affectionately known as Evita.

9 Bértola and Ocampo, *Economic Development*, p. 192.

10 Rostow summarizes modernization theory in "The Stages of Economic Growth."

11 Neo-Marxists, like Andrés Gunder Frank, advocated that underdevelopment was a counterpart of development in capitalist, First World, countries.

12 Celso Furtado was a prominent ECLA economist who espoused a more complex approach to structural change. His ideas impacted the entire region, but particularly in his native country, Brazil.

13 Cuba, for example, produced only eight films between 1941 and 1945 and Chile just a few more.

14 This increase in military production coincided with Brazil's military dictatorship from 1964–1985.

15 Galeano, *Open Veins of Latin America*, p. 263.

16 The book was translated into multiple languages, selling over one million copies since it was first published in 1971. Larry Rohter, "Author Changes his Mind on '70s Manifesto." *New York Times*, May 23, 2014.

17 Cuba had the fourth highest GDP per capita in Latin America in 1920 but lagged after protectionist measures were imposed. Bértola and Ocampo, *Economic Development*, p. 16.

18 The compromise saw Soviets agree to keep nuclear missiles out of Cuba and the United States agree to remove nuclear missiles from Turkey.

19 Fidel Castro served as Cuba's prime minister through 1976 and as Cuba's president from 1976–2008.

20 Castillo Bueno, *Reyita*, p. 119.

21 Bulmer-Thomas, *Economic History*, 3rd edition, p. 336.

22 Additional inspiration came from East Asian countries that had implemented land reform and seemed to be outperforming Latin America.

23 To help understand the scale, Cárdenas's land reform was the equivalent of a US president appropriating the equivalent of all the farmland in 1940 California and Virginia. United States Department of Agriculture. National Agricultural Statistics Service, *1940 Agricultural Census*, https://agcensus.library.cornell.edu/census_year/1940-census/.

24 Bértola and Ocampo, *Economic Development*, p. 196.

25 Holden and Zolov, *Latin America and the United States*, chapter 4.

26 Allende himself was a Marxist but was elected on a multi-party ticket. Pinochet was not ousted, but rather voted out in a plebiscite and became a senator for life.

27 Acosta Matos, Eliades, ed. *La Dictadura de Trujillo: Documentos (1950–1961 Tomo III)*, Volume 5. Santo Domingo: Archivo General de la Nación, Editora Búho, 2012, pp. 178–80. http://www.latinamericanstudies.org/book/dictadura_de_trujillo_v5.pdf.

28 Bértola and Ocampo, *Economic Development*, pp. 175–76; table is citing Maddison, *The World Economy*.

29 Reimers, "Education and Social Progress," p. 440.

30 At the start of the Literacy Campaign, Cuba's adult illiteracy rate was roughly 25 percent.

31 Astorga, Bergés, and Fitzgerald, "Standard of Living," p. 790.

32 ECLAC, *Anuário Estadístico*, table 32–34. For Chileans, 33.3 percent of the economically active population had between 10 and 12 years of schooling.

33 US Bureau of the Census, Current Population Reports, Series P-20, No. 390, *Educational Attainment in the United States: March 1981 and 1980*, Washington DC: US Government Printing Office, 1984. https://www2.census.gov/programs-surveys/demo/tables/educational-attainment/time-series/p20-390/tab-06.pdf.
34 ELCAC, *Anuário Estadístico*, table 11. Countries with life expectancies over 70 included Costa Rica (73.5), Cuba (74.2), Chile (71.0), Panama (71.1), and Uruguay (70.9). Life expectancies were lower than 60 years in Bolivia (50.7), Guatemala (59.0), Haiti (52.7), Nicaragua (59.8), and Peru (58.6).
35 In 1970, 62 percent of working women were employed in the service sector. That share increased to 65 percent by 1980.
36 Two-thirds of Haitian working women were employed in the agricultural sector. Fertility rates and female labor participation, ECLAC, *Anuário Estadístico*, tables 12, 15, and 16.
37 The ability of filmmakers to critique the state quo, ironically, was only possible because of state-led support for national film industries.
38 Lula was a founding member of Brazil's Worker's Party and would be elected as Brazil's president in 2002, 2006, and again in 2022.
39 US banks had 60 percent of loans earmarked for "general purpose," Bulmer-Thomas, *Economic History*, 3rd edition, p. 387.
40 During the first oil crisis in 1973, foreign direct investment in the region for oil- and non-oil-producing countries alike increased. The recession that the second crisis precipitated, however, led to increasing interest rates.
41 A selection of Domitila Barrios de Chungara's *Let Me Speak!* appears in *The Bolivia Reader*, pp. 452–59.

Suggested Media, Literature, and Digital Resources

Castillo Bueno, María de los Reyes, with Daisy Rubiera Castillo. *Reyita: The Life of a Black Cuban Woman in the Twentieth Century*. Durham: Duke University Press, 2000.

Economic Commission for Latin America and the Caribbean. "About." Accessed January 24, 2024. https://www.cepal.org/en/about.

Economic Commission for Latin America and the Caribbean. "CEPALSTAT: Bases de Datos y Publicaciones Estadísticas." Accessed January 24, 2024. https://statistics.cepal.org/portal/cepalstat/index.html.

Guevara, Che. *The Motorcycle Diaries: A Journey Around South America*. Translated by Ann Wright. London: Verso, 1995.

Gutiérrez, Gustavo. *A Theology of Liberation: History, Politics, and Salvation*. Maryknoll: Orbis Books, 1988.

Holden, Robert H., and Eric. Zolov. *Latin America and the United States: A Documentary History*, 2nd edition. New York: Oxford University Press, 2011.

Jesus, Carolina Maria de. *Child of the Dark: The Diary of Carolina Maria de Jesus*. Translated by David St. Clair, centennial edition. New York: Signet Classics, 2018.

Lins, Paulo, and Alison Entrekin. *City of God*, 1st American ed. New York: Black Cat, 2006.

Murphy, Catherine. *Maestra*. San Francisco: Women Make Movies, 2018.

National Security Archive. "Virtual Reading Room." Accessed January 24, 2024. https://nsarchive.gwu.edu/virtual-reading-room.

"La nueva canción: The New Song Movement in South America." Smithsonian Folkways Recordings. Accessed January 24, 2024. https://folkways.si.edu/

la-nueva-cancion-new-song-movement-south-america/latin-world-struggle-protest/music/article/smithsonian.
Rocha, Glauber, Luiz Augusto Mendes, Yoná Magalhães, Othon Bastos, Mauricio do Valle, Lidio Silva, Sonia dos Humildes, and Geraldo del Rey. *Deus e o Diabo na Terra do Sol*, edição definitiva. São Paulo: Versátil Home Video, 2003.

Select Bibliography

Abreu, Marcelo P. de, Afonso S. Bevilaqua, and Demosthenes M. Pinho. "Import Substitution and Growth in Brazil, 1890s–1970s." In *An Economic History of Twentieth-Century Latin America: Volume 3: Industrialization and the State in Latin America: The Postwar Years*, 154–75. London: Palgrave Macmillan UK, 2000.
Astorga, Pablo, Ame R. Bergés, and Valpy FitzGerald. "The Standard of Living in Latin America during the Twentieth Century." *The Economic History Review* 58, no. 4 (2005): 765–96.
Bértola, Luis, and José Antonio Ocampo. *The Economic Development of Latin America since Independence*. Oxford: Oxford University Press, 2012.
Bleynat, Ingrid. *Vendors' Capitalism: A Political Economy of Public Markets in Mexico City*. Redwood City: Stanford University Press, 2021. https://doi.org/10.1515/9781503628304.
Brender, Valerie. "Economic Transformations in Chile: The Formation of the Chicago Boys." *The American Economist* 55, no. 1 (2010): 111–22.
Brune, Krista. "Subversive Instruments: Protest and Politics of MPB and the Nueva Canción." *Studies in Latin American Popular Culture* 33 (2015): 128–45. https://doi.org/10.7560/SLAPC3309.
Cárdenas, Enrique. "The Process of Accelerated Industrialization in Mexico, 1929–82." In *An Economic History of Twentieth-Century Latin America: Volume 3: Industrialization and the State in Latin America: The Postwar Years, 176-204*. London: Palgrave Macmillan UK, 2000.
Bulmer-Thomas, Victor. *The Political Economy of Central America since 1920*. Cambridge: Cambridge University Press, 1987.
Bulmer-Thomas, Victor. *The Economic History of Latin America since Independence*, Third edition. New York: Cambridge University Press, 2014
Cardoso, Fernando Henrique, and Enzo Faletto. *Dependencia y Desarrollo en América Latina*. Mexico City: Siglo XXI, 1971.
Chonchol, Jacques. *Sistemas Agrarios en América Latina*. Mexico City: Fondo de Cultura Económica, 1994.
Díaz Alejandro, Carlos F. "Latin America in the 1930s." In *Latin America in the 1930s: The Role of the Periphery in World Crisis*, edited by Rosemary Thorp. London: Palgrave Macmillan, 1984. https://doi.org/10.1007/978-1-349-17554-3.
Díaz Fuentes, Daniel. "Latin America during the Interwar Period: The Rise and Fall of the Gold Standard in Argentina, Brazil, and Mexico." In *Latin America and the World Economy Since 1800*, edited by John H. Coatsworth and Alan M. Taylor, 443–70. Cambridge: Harvard University Press, 1998.
Eaglin, Jennifer. *Sweet Fuel: A Political and Environmental History of Brazilian Ethanol*. New York: Oxford University Press, 2022.
Eckstein, Susan. "Dollarization and Its Discontents: Remittances and the Remaking of Cuba in the Post-Soviet Era." *Comparative Politics* 36, no. 3 (2004): 313–30. https://doi.org/10.2307/4150133.

ECLAC. *Anuário Estadístico de América Latina y el Caribe*. Santiago: ECLAC, 1990.
ECLAC. *ECLAC 40 Years (1948–1988)*. Santiago: United Nations, 1988.
Eichengreen, Barry, and Richard Portes. "After the Deluge: Default, Negotiation and Readjustment during the Interwar Years." In *The International Debt Crisis in Historical Perspective*, 12–47. Cambridge: MIT Press, 1989.
Farjado, Margarita. *The World that Latin America Created: The United Nations Economic Commission for Latin America in the Development Era*. Cambridge: Harvard University Press, 2021.
FitzGerald, Edmund Valpy Knox. "ECLA and the Theory of Import-Substituting Industrialization in Latin America." In *Economic History of Twentieth Century Latin America, Volume 3*, edited by Enrique Cárdenas, Jose Antonio Ocampo, and Rosemary Thorp. Basingstoke: Palgrave, 2000.
Fontes, Paulo, and Francisco Barbosa De Macedo. "Strikes and Pickets in Brazil: Working-Class Mobilization in the 'Old' and 'New' Unionism, the Strikes of 1957 and 1980." *International Labor and Working-Class History* 83 (2013): 86–111.
Frank, Andre Gunder. *The Development of Underdevelopment*. Boston: New England Free Press, 1969.
Frankema, Ewout. *Has Latin America Always Been Unequal? A Comparative Study of Asset and Income Inequality in the Long Twentieth Century*. Leiden: Brill, 2009.
Furtado, Celso. *Economic Development of Latin America: A Survey from Colonial Times to the Cuban Revolution*. Cambridge: Cambridge University Press, 1970.
Galeano, Eduardo. *Open Veins of Latin America: Five Centuries of the Pillage of a Continent*. Translated by Cedric Belfrage. New York City: New York University Press, 1997.
García, Manuel, and Victor Tokman. "Changes in Employment and Crisis." *CEPAL Review*, 24 (1984): 103–15.
García, Sandra C. Mendiola. *Street democracy: Vendors, violence, and public space in Late Twentieth-Century Mexico*. Lincoln: University of Nebraska Press, 2017.
Gomes, Caio. "Nueva Canción." Translated by Eoin O'Neill. *On Trans Atlantic Cultures*. April 2022. https://doi.org/10.35008/tracs-0229.
Haber, Stephen H. "Business Enterprise and the Great Depression in Brazil: A Study of Profits and Losses in Textile Manufacturing." *Business History Review* 66, no. 2 (1992): 335–63.
———. "The Political Economy of Industrialization." In *The Cambridge Economic History of Latin America. Volume II. The Long Twentieth Century*, edited by Victor Bulmer-Thomas, John H. Coatsworth, and Roberto Cortés Conde, 537–84. New York: Cambridge University Press, 2006.
Hirschman, Albert O. "The Political Economy of Import-Substituting Industrialization in Latin America." *The Quarterly Journal of Economics* 82, no. 1 (1968): 1–32.
———. "The Political Economy of Latin American Development: Seven Exercises in Retrospection." *Latin American Research Review* 22, no. 3 (1987): 7–36.
Irwin, Robert McKee, Maricruz Castro, Mónica Szurmuk, Inmaculada Gordillo Alvarez, and Dubravka Suznjevic. *Global Mexican Cinema: Its Golden Age: "El Cine Mexicano Se Impone."* London: Palgrave Macmillan, 2013.
King, John. *Magical Reels: A History of Cinema in Latin America*. London: Verso, 1990.

Kornbluh, Peter. *The Pinochet File: A Declassified Dossier on Atrocity and Accountability*. New York: The New Press, 2016.
Love, Joseph L. "Economic Ideas and Ideologies in Latin America Since 1930." In *The Cambridge History of Latin America, Volume 6: Latin America: Economy and Society since 1930*, edited by Leslie Bethell. Cambridge: Cambridge University Press, 1994.
Maddison, Angus. *The World Economy: A Millennial Perspective*. Paris: OECD Development Centre, 2001.
Mesa-Lago, Carmelo. *Social Security in Latin America: Pressure Groups, Stratification, and Inequality*. Pittsburgh: University of Pittsburgh Press, 1978.
Pons, Frank Moya. "Import-Substitution Industrialization Policies in the Dominican Republic, 1925–61." *The Hispanic American Historical Review* 70, no. 4 (1990): 539–77. https://doi.org/10.1215/00182168-70.4.539
Reimers, Fernando. "Education and Social Progress." In *The Cambridge Economic History of Latin America. Volume II. The Long Twentieth Century*, edited by Victor Bulmer-Thomas, John H. Coatsworth, and Roberto Cortés Conde, 427–80. New York: Cambridge University Press, 2006.
Rios, Palmira. "Export-Oriented Industrialization and the Demand for Female Labor: Puerto Rican Women in the Manufacturing Sector, 1952–1980." *Gender and Society* 4, no. 3 (1990): 321–37.
Rostow, Walt Whitman. "The Stages of Economic Growth." *Economic History Review* (1959): 1–16.
Santamaria, A. "Dos siglos de especialización y dos décadas de incertidumbre: La historia económica de Cuba, 1800–2010." In *Institucionalidad y Desarrollo Económico en América Latina*, edited by Luis Bértocla and Pablo Gerchunoff, 135–90. Santiago de Chile: ECLAC and AECID, 2011.
Solbrig, Otto T. "Structure, Performance and Policy in Agriculture." In *The Cambridge Economic History of Latin America. Volume II. The Long Twentieth Century*, edited by Victor Bulmer-Thomas, John H. Coatsworth, and Roberto Cortés Conde, 483–536. New York: Cambridge University Press, 2006.
Thomson, Sinclair, et al., eds. *The Bolivia Reader: History, Culture, Politics*. Durham: Duke University Press, 2018.
Thorp, Rosemary. *Latin America in the 1930s: The Role of the Periphery in World Crisis*. London: Macmillan, 1984.
Tinsman, Heidi. "Struggles in the Countryside: Gender Politics and Agrarian Reform in Democracy and Dictatorship." *Radical History Review* 124 (2016): 67–76.
Vergara, Angela. "Revisiting Pampa Irigoin: Social Movements, Repression, and Political Culture in 1960s Chile." *Radical History Review* 124 (2016): 43–54.
Woodard, James. *Brazil's Revolution in Commerce: Creating Consumer Capitalism in the American Century*. Chapel Hill: University of North Carolina Press, 2020.

6 The Market Return (1980–2008)

Latin America faced one of its greatest volatility challenges in the penultimate decade of the twentieth century. Like the other periods of transition detailed in this book, the region's approach to achieving growth and development changed substantially. The state-led period (1930–1980) was largely dismantled and a new market-driven approach emerged by 1985. As inflation raged, state-owned enterprises were sold, and budgets were balanced. The reforms instituted to make this transition are often referred to as the Washington Consensus and are characterized as "neoliberal," or free-market reforms. Many of them were, but the state was never fully extricated from the playing field, and the process was much more complex. For example, trade reforms often embodied open regionalism rather than complete liberalization, and as democracy returned to the region in the 1990s, governments increased social spending, raising taxes to keep deficits low.

The origin of these reforms derived from a variety of sources. An external disruption, the **1979 Volcker Shock**, and the subsequent 1982 Mexican Peso Crisis precipitated the about-face. Homegrown discontent with Latin America's response to the shock, especially in comparison to East Asian economies like Thailand and South Korea, found Latin Americans entertaining alternatives to the inward-looking state-led model. Outside forces, mostly the creditors that Latin America owed money to, extended a tantalizing offer of debt restructuring if economic austerity measures were implemented. Latin American leaders, desperate to escape the recession and regression and thinking the downturn would be temporary, began to accept the terms. Instead, the 1980s became known as Latin America's "Lost Decade," and it took a full 25 years for the region to recover from its losses.

By the 1990s, as capital began to return to the region, it was trade liberalization through preferential trade agreements and trading blocs that took center stage. Typified by the **1994 North American Free Trade Agreement (NAFTA)**, countries hoped to become more competitive globally and to

DOI: 10.4324/9781003283843-6

reconstruct the losses from the 1980s. The results did lead to moderate growth as global trade increased, but the New Economic Model had its shortcomings. Productivity gains were lackluster, and growth was often accompanied by underemployment and migration challenges. The economic changes also did little to address underlying income and socio-economic inequality, and many currencies remained susceptible to volatility, vulnerabilities exposed by the **1997 East Asian financial crisis**. Once commodity markets bounced back in the early twenty-first century, voters had elected leaders with social priorities that engaged marginalized groups. Macroeconomic policies largely continued to follow a market-driven path, but how revenues were spent in democratic governments began to reflect societal needs.

Volcker Shock, 1979 (Washington, DC, United States) and 1982 Pesos Crisis (Mexico City, Mexico)

In 1979, the inflation that sent Brazilians and Latin Americans to the picket lines also reared its head in the United States. US inflation rates reached an average of over 11 percent and rates for transportation and housing were even higher. This increase proved particularly burdensome for the poor and working class. In an effort to cool off rising inflation amidst increased oil prices, the United States Federal Reserve chairmen Paul Volcker increased interest rates (in similar fashion as other OECD countries).[1] This would become known as the Volcker Shock. At the time of the shock, Latin America was the most highly indebted developing region to the United States: over half of private debt loans issued between 1973 and 1981 went to the region. The decade that followed, the 1980s, would become known as the **Lost Decade** in Latin America. It was characterized not just by a *dramatic reversal of growth and development, but as countries struggled to make interest payments and worked to reschedule debts, citizens bore the brunt of the resulting increases in poverty rates, inequality, informality, violence, and inflation*. Much more detrimental than the Great Depression, the 1980s shook Latin America to its core, initiating a move away from a state-led toward a market-driven economic approach.

The region's vulnerability came to a head in 1982 in Mexico. As an oil-producing country, Mexico had increased oil exports in the 1970s during the 1973 and 1978 oil crises. To do so, Petróleos Mexicanos, PEMEX, a state-owned enterprise, required importing capital goods needed to extract oil. In the balance of trade, Mexico continued to import more than they exported, and they took out more loans to pay for this new machinery. As interest rates rose after the Volcker Shock, and oil prices fell lower than expected during the 1980s global recession, Mexico was on the precipice of a crisis. Intensifying Mexico's precarity was the fact that many *Mexican investors began turning toward US banks as an alternative and more secure investment opportunity*. As Mexican investors sought out US dollars as a more reliable currency, this **capital flight** made the value of the Mexican peso decline. In 1982, the situation culminated in Mexico devaluing its peso, which lost 60 percent of its purchasing power. This set off a downward spiral of further dollar flight followed by further devaluations, plunging Mexico into a recession and making timely debt payments to its creditors simply impossible.

The impact of the financial crisis and default expanded well beyond Mexico as foreign banks seemed to suddenly become wary of the entire region's ability to meet interest payments on debts issued in the 1970s. The fact that many currencies were overvalued brought the fear that "anywhere" could become the next Mexico. Each country had a unique set of exports and macroeconomic policies, but in general countries had high external debt obligations relative to domestic production. This high debt-to-GDP ratio put Latin American governments at risk of defaulting on loan and interest payments. Exacerbating the rising interest rates was the fact that oil's low price was not anomalous: most global commodity prices fell. Latin American nations had somewhat diversified production during the state-led period, but export commodities remained important components of GDP. While low export prices continued, and rising interest rates ensured that debt payments would increase, the debt-to-GDP ratio continue to rise.

In the immediate aftermath of the peso crisis, the prevailing opinion was that the downturn was temporary, and that the region needed more access to funds to weather the downturn. Both countries and lenders looked to **reschedule debt** as a solution. Over one-quarter of loans to Latin America had variable interest rates, so the hope was *that decreasing the amount paid and extending the payment period would free up enough capital so that the countries could make payments* and would also open a flow of new loans to the region. Understanding rescheduling on an individual level is helpful in conceptualizing the structure. Imagine having a large student loan payment that you are suddenly unable to pay because of something like a change in your job or another major life circumstance. You can either stop making payments, or you can reach out to the loan company to see if you can decrease your monthly payments. The latter will require a change in the terms of the loan that will extend the length of time (months) you will be making payments and might require accepting a different interest rate, but it will preserve your ability to borrow money in the future. When your circumstances improve, you could once again increase your payments, if you choose. For the lender, restructuring increases the likelihood of being paid at all, even if the wait to be paid extends. But lenders to Latin America were wary of the region, so creditors added debt rescheduling stipulations that required countries to implement macroeconomic discipline and policy reform that included cutting government spending and increasing foreign currency reserves.

Latin Americans, eager to return to normalcy and to continue growing the economy, accepted the unequal terms, thinking that the downturn was temporary. But it was not temporary. Global commodity prices remained low and new credit failed to return to the region, plunging Latin America even further into duress. Governments tried to improve the balance of trade, but under the new debt stipulations and in the absence of new loans, heavy government spending was not an option. Thus, they returned to restricting imports and incentivizing exports through lower export taxes. The strategy backfired: lower export taxes brought in even less revenue and import restrictions seriously constrained regional trade, further crippling national budgets.

In September 1985, the International Monetary Fund (IMF) proposed a more intentional approach, recognizing the unlikelihood of a quick recovery. The plan, known as the Baker Plan, would begin to ration money and loans to countries. It prevented Latin American countries from raising the debt ceiling, requiring them to balance national budgets and implement austerity measures to receive the desperately needed IMF money. Ultimately, the restructuring marked the end of the state-led period of growth and a move toward a market-based approach. The United States, as a leading stakeholder in monetary lending to Latin America, held a significant role in the plan. Approval of the Baker Plan, and the 1989 Brady Plan that followed, was contingent on the approval not just of the IMF, the World Bank, and groups of international bankers, but also of both the United States Treasury and Federal Reserve.

The multitude of trade and financial reforms introduced over the course of the 1980s into Latin American economies would eventually become known as the **Washington Consensus**. It included measures that would *liberalize trade and restrict tariffs that had inched up over the state-led period, allowing for competition. It also included financial reforms that worked toward stability through correct exchange rates and balancing budgets, and required privatizing and auctioning off many of the state-owned enterprises*. It goes without saying that anti-communism was also a prerequisite for lending and restructuring, meaning that Nicaragua under the control of the Sandinistas and embroiled in civil war, was unable to renegotiate debt payments. The degree of implementation varied, but most countries took significant strides toward a market approach. Even Cuba, decidedly not part of the Washington Consensus reforms, had to reevaluate its economy after the fall of the Soviet Union. The island nation transitioned to relying more heavily on foreign tourism and implemented a tourist economy with different price structures to operate alongside a national economy. Sometimes these reforms are critiqued as originating outside of Latin

America, but Latin American states were also heavily involved in the process, desperately wanting to reduce the share of national budgets going toward interest payments, which reached 2–4 percent by 1982.

Restructuring did not see an immediate return of capital into the region and the 1980s represented a severe setback for Latin America. Commodity export prices continued to decline, so countries continued to struggle with a high debt-to-GDP ratio. In every economic indicator the region struggled. Globally, Latin America's share of worldwide production also fell. Debt payments as a share of GPD peaked in 1985 and 1986, but by 1990 still represented 10 percent of national budgets.[2] GDP per capita fell by as much as 8 percent as inflation rose. Inflation reached triple digits in Argentina, Bolivia, Brazil, Nicaragua, and Peru. Rates rose as high as 8,000 percent in Bolivia in 1985 and 33,000 percent in Nicaragua in 1988. Hyperinflation of the 1980s had the ability to change consumer spending habits: rather than save for a rainy day, it was more valuable to spend in the moment. Only Panama and Colombia were spared the worst. Much of Colombia's relative stability was bolstered by an influx of dollars connected to illegal drug trafficking that did not reflect on the balance of payments, and in Panama, the lone country with a dollar economy, offshore banking, which also included money laundering, provided the country with much-needed foreign reserves.

The reforms also came with additional social pains. The new debt agreements limited governments' ability to spend on social programs like schools, hospitals, and infrastructure. As national currencies were devalued (often multiple times), people's savings evaporated overnight. In the wake of this, confidence in domestic banks and savings eroded: many people preferred to save away dollars under a mattress for the next crisis, rather than risk putting national currencies in a bank to lose value. For the working class, a devalued currency meant wages shifted downward, eroding minimum wage increases earned in the 1970s. The decrease in real wages ranged between 20 and 40 percent, and many in the urban working class stared poverty in the face with little recourse (see Figure 6.1). Regionally, moderate and extreme poverty had decreased considerably in the 1970s, but the 1980s saw an about-face with a 54 percent increase in moderate poverty and a 37 percent increase in extreme poverty. Within such turbulent challenges and funding cuts for safety maintenance and police patrols, violence in the region increased.

Faced with such dire prospects, many urban residents turned to informality. During the 1980s, Latin America's informal employment rate more than doubled, representing 42 percent of the workforce in 1990. Informality was costly for both workers and governments. For workers, informality rarely provided the safety net of pensions, worker compensation, collective bargaining, and vacation time that formal sector

Figure 6.1 Facing economic challenges and political repression in the 1980s, women in "La Victoria," an informal settlement in Santiago, Chile, used the collective *olla común*, the common pot, to confront hunger. "Olla Común" La Victoria. By Paulo Slachevsky, CC BY-SA 4.0, Wikimedia Commons.

jobs offered. For governments, the informal sector largely did not pay taxes, rendering absent a large portion of potential government revenue. Compounding the increasing informality was the myriad government regulations and bureaucratic steps needed to start a legitimate business. While the Washington Consensus may have addressed macroeconomic policies, it did not call for dismantling the painstaking bureaucratic processes needed to create formal housing, transportation, or businesses. For example, to legally open a small store in Lima in the 1980s required 43 days of bureaucratic paperwork and paying over 15 times the monthly living wage.[3] Facing such barriers, informal businesses often proved more attractive to entrepreneurs, despite the fact that they would never be able to accrue pension plans offered by formal employment.

It should come as no surprise that another common reaction to the dire economic situation of this period was migration. Early on, alongside investments, many middle-class Latin Americans left for Europe and the United States, and in Brazil and Peru, Japanese descendants moved to Japan. They took with them not only their skills and experience, but also their money. For many Mexicans, the United States served as a beacon. The proximity of the US border, combined with established Mexican-American communities throughout the country, particularly along the border, in most major US cities, and in much of the Southwest and Texas, served as an additional draw.[4] In 1980, roughly 2.2 million Mexicans were living in the United States, and it is estimated that half were undocumented.[5] By 1990, Mexican immigrant rates almost doubled, reaching close to 4.3 million. Undocumented rates also continued to swell.[6] The share of Caribbean and Central American migrations to the United States also increased during this period. Economic opportunity was the prime motivator, but many Central Americans and Haitians sought refuge from the political violence ravaging their countries.[7]

The United States was not the sole destination for migrants. Similar corridors developed to other countries with better performing economies. Caught up in a paramilitary-narco war, many rural Colombians moved to Venezuela and Ecuador. Facing ethnic discrimination and few prospects, Bolivians joined compatriots who had moved to Brazil in the preceding decade. In Cuba, following a severe economic downturn and a dramatic situation whereby 10,000 Cubans took refuge in the Peruvian embassy, Castro organized the Mariel boatlift to allow Cubans wanting to leave the island freedom to emigrate if somebody was willing to pick them up. Between April and October of 1980, roughly 100,000 Cubans (and 25,000 Haitians capitalizing on the agreement) arrived in the United States.

Economic instability did not just impact migration; it also disrupted the existing politics. The economic downturn proved destabilizing enough to help topple or at least severely tarnish the existing political structures, many of which were right-wing military regimes. It marked the end of the Duvalier regimes in Haiti, which had included secret terror squads and incredible state violence. By the middle of the 1980s, the Argentine, Brazilian, and Uruguayan dictatorships had ended. Those in Chile and Paraguay had fallen by the end of the decade. The global recession and domestic hardships in the United States also brought increased scrutiny to US military and economic aid being sent to what were effectively Cold War initiatives in Central America. Although never fully resolved, civil conflicts in El Salvador, Nicaragua, and Guatemala petered out as the 1990s dawned.

The 1980s was not a loss for everyone in the region. For some connected and well-positioned individuals, the decade provided an opportunity to buy the auctioned-off state-owned enterprises at an incredibly discounted rate. SOEs (see Chapter 5) came under particular scrutiny because most operated inefficiently and required continual national and international loans. Employing tens of thousands of workers, SOEs were costly, especially if those workers were inefficient. The fiscal conservatism of the Washington Consensus required privatizing many SOEs. From industrial firms and public service companies to telecommunications, there was not even a clear count of how many SOEs existed by 1985. In Brazil, for example, the government claimed 175 SOEs existed, but one estimate put the number much higher: 200 national, 339 state, and 32 municipal SOEs. Between 1985 and 1992 over 2,000 SOEs were privatized in Latin America.[8] Governments often maintained some form of shareholding in these companies, but not as the majority investor controlling over 50 percent of the company.

As state-owned companies were often sold off at a discounted rate, they became tantalizing opportunities for investors. Those ventures that paid off created a highly elite business class. Carlos Slim offers a case in point. In 1990, the Mexican government agreed to auction off the state phone company, TELMEX. Carlos Slim, an established businessman, bought the company for just 20 percent of its estimated value. It was the culmination of a number of similar investments he made during the 1980s privatizations, and it was one that would make him one of the world's richest men in the twenty-first century. This was the embodiment of the Baker Plan's goals: eliminate excess spending, stimulate investment within Latin America, and make profitable enterprises that would eventually serve to provide jobs and stabilize the economy.

Did this market-driven approach provide the jobs and stability that it promised? The initial austerity measures of the 1980s had extreme consequences for some of the most marginalized individuals, but the 1990s brought some improvements. Somewhat aided by further debt restructuring under the 1989 Brady Plan, but mostly by a return of investment in the region, governments could begin to reconstruct confidence in their economic policies and financial systems. Recovery was slow going, and it would not be for another quarter of a century that the region would reach pre-1980 measures. The more moderate pace, however, was perhaps a marker of reduced volatility, something that had perpetually eluded the region.

North American Free Trade Agreement, 1994 (Mexico, United States, Canada)

It was December 31, 1993, when the state capital of Chiapas, Mexico, San Cristóbal de las Casas, was taken over without bloodshed. The *Zapatistas*, a group of leftist-organized Mayan communities who were armed, issued a declaration of war against Mexico, urging Mexicans to overthrow the federal government and the army. They timed the takeover to shock international audiences as it coincided with hemispheric celebration of the **North American Free Trade Agreement (NAFTA)**.[9] Signed as an agreement between *Canada, Mexico, and the United States, NAFTA was promoted as having the ability to stimulate trade between the three countries by working toward the free flow of electronics, industrial equipment, cars, luxury* *goods, and produce across the three countries' borders.* The approach was to eliminate tariffs and quotas piecemeal and to eliminate trade barriers by 2008. NAFTA was designed to create an international market able to compete with China and the European Union. Such trade was valued at US $6.5 trillion and encompassed the lives of 370 million people. The Mexican government had initiated the conversation to expand an existing US-Canadian agreement to include their southern neighbor and celebrated the agreement as an opportunity for the Mexican economy and wages to grow, something desperately needed coming out of the 1980s. Both the United States and Mexico also hoped that improving Mexico's economic situation would incentivize Mexicans to remain in the country rather than migrate north.

The Zapatistas saw NAFTA as a continuation of the market-oriented reforms laying siege to the cultural basis of their Indigenous identity. Building on the Washington Consensus, Mexican President Carlos Salinas de Gortari issued an executive order in 1992 that allowed for Indigenous communal lands to be partitioned and privatized. For the over three million households living on 28,000 rural *ejidos*, communal lands, the order came as a shock. This included many of the Zapatistas, who, instead of turning to migration or idly watching, took up arms and invoked the name of Mexico revolutionary Emiliano Zapata in an act of resistance.

NAFTA faced significant pushback in Mexico amongst the Zapatistas, but it was far from the only free or liberalized trade agreement in the region. By the mid-1980s, when it became clear that the economic downturn was not temporary, the region turned away from the ECLA structuralist model toward a market-driven strategy that looked to reduce trade barriers such as quotas and tariffs. By 2000, all Latin American countries had joined the World Trade Organization (WTO), the successor to the General Agreement on Tariffs and Trade (GATT) established after World War II.[10] Countries also joined *smaller agreements working toward open regionalism and the free movement of goods, services, and factors of production.* **Preferential trade agreements**, which were n*egotiated between two (or a few) independent countries*, were common. Chile led the way in this style of agreement, being part of 25 trade agreements covering 64 markets spanning from Colombia and Canada to Turkey, Thailand, Malaysia, and beyond by 2018.

Trade blocs, where multiple countries joined a trade agreement that reduced trade barriers between them to encourage open regionalism, were also common. The idea was to incentivize regional development by promoting trade within the region. Having low regional tariffs would encourage this exchange of goods. Trading blocs also had the benefit of being able to better negotiate globally, an imperative given the rising prominence of Chinese and Southeast Asian markets. Regional trade had gained some traction in the 1960s when the Andean Community and the Central American Common Market were formed, but these groups found renewed interest and popularity in the market-driven era.[11] The hopes were that this market-driven approach would stimulate development and address the regional inequalities between larger and smaller countries.

In 1980, the Latin American Integration Association (ALADI) formed to promote regional development through preferential regional tariffs in the hopes of moving toward a common market similar to the European Union. ALADI registered the region's trade blocs, such as Mercosur, which became an operational trade bloc in 1991 and initially included Argentina, Brazil, Uruguay, and Paraguay. In 1998, Mercosur and the Andean Community began negotiating a South American Free Trade Area. Then, in 2006, DR-CAFTA brought together Central America and the Dominican Republic and the United States. The Pacific Alliance trade bloc, which included Chile, Colombia, Mexico, and Peru, formed in 2011. By that time, Panama, Mexico, and Cuba, along with South America's ten "Latin" American countries, were all members of ALADI. As of 2022, Central American countries (except Panama) were not ALADI members, but they did belong to the Central American Integration System, formed in 1991, and which included the Dominican Republic, Panama, and Belize.[12] The lone country in the region without a free trade or preferential trade agreement within Latin America was Haiti. While a member of the WTO and the Caribbean Community (dominated by Anglophone countries), Haiti was once again isolated from the region.

As of 2022, true open regionalism had not been obtained. Trade barriers in the forms of quotas and tariffs were reduced with a careful dismantling of the "geologic" layers of protection built up over years, but there is no single currency, and labor movement is restricted. Furthermore, dismantling or altering domestic policies, which are also necessary to liberalize trade, requires difficult and almost impossible political negotiations. As a case in point, one of the reasons the Free Trade Area of the Americas (FTAA) stalled in 2005 was because the United States, facing a powerful domestic farm lobby, was unwilling to cede to Mercosur's calls to reduce subsidies to US farmers and agricultural exporters. Without a reduction, Mercosur exports that competed with American exports, like Argentine wheat and Brazilian oranges, would be starting at a competitive disadvantage. Proof of the challenges that could occur required looking no further than the short-term impact NAFTA had on Mexican corn production.

After NAFTA, Mexico became the leading trading partner of the United States, representing 60 percent of the trade between the United States and Latin America. One of the products Mexico began importing from the United States was corn. An iconic staple of Mexico's agricultural production since the pre-colonial period, US yellow corn, used for animal feed and industrial use, was cheaper than the Mexican equivalent because it was heavily subsidized by the US government. While Mexico's white corn production survived and eventually increased (white corn is largely for human consumption), its market growth was much less substantial than yellow corn's. Furthermore, while eventually Mexico's corn production stabilized, for the two million people employed in the agricultural sector who lost their jobs and the millions of others who received lower wages or were underemployed in the immediate aftermath, NAFTA brought suffering and did little to relieve poverty.[13]

Complaints about NAFTA also emerged in the industrial sector. Mexico paid lower wages, so many United States firms moved industrial production to Mexico. For many people in the United States, this did not have a significant, immediate impact and had the potential to lower the cost of items that once assembled in Mexico could be sold in the United States. For employees in manufacturing companies that relocated, like car manufacturers in Detroit, or even car carpet companies in upstate South Carolina, NAFTA created pockets of extreme impact in the United States. For the Mexican communities where these semi-skilled and skilled jobs transferred, NAFTA also created pockets of extreme opportunity.

Most growth in the manufacturing section in Mexico, however, was related to the **maquiladora** sector. *These low-tech assembly plants take advantage of lower cost labor and use imported inputs to create finished products that are then exported and sold at lower prices to a consumer.* Maquiladoras had existed as early as the 1960s and could be located in a multitude of countries, but trade liberalization in the 1980s created the fertile environment for their explosion. This was particularly the case in Mexico. With the introduction of NAFTA, maquiladoras grew from 455 with 130,000 workers in 1982 to over 2,000 employing over 600,000 workers (two-thirds of whom were women) in 1998. Assembling products like televisions and radios, maquiladoras operated with minimal oversight to ensure that labor laws were being followed. Workers often earned below minimum wage in unsafe working conditions and women's reproductive rights were also exploited. Fertility was policed to prevent owners from having to provide maternity leave and maquiladoras also became magnets for feminicides and gender violence, as women returning from late-night shifts became targets along the United States/Mexico border.[14]

Whereas NAFTA and the liberalized trade agreements worked toward barrier-free exchange of goods, the logic did not extend to individuals, as workers. In fact, one selling point of NAFTA was that it would slow unauthorized immigration of Mexicans into the United Sates by creating jobs in Mexico. The impact was the opposite: many Mexican agricultural jobs disappeared. This came on the heels of another Mexican currency crisis and peso devaluation in 1994. This currency crisis led to another financial crisis, commonly referred to as the Tequila Crisis, which eroded Mexican real wages and had international reverberations. Coupled with skepticism about the Mexican government (the leading presidential candidate was assassinated there in 1994), Mexicans were just as likely to migrate without authorization after NAFTA as they were before, and Mexican migration to the United States peaked in 2007. However, the increased tightening of US immigration policies and enforcement meant that fewer immigrants returned, leading to a subsequent increase in the resident Mexican population in the United States.

Trade liberalization's impact on agricultural jobs and failure to address underemployment served to increase out-migration in Latin America. Migrants in the 1990s, however, often benefited from social networks and immigrant communities established during the 1980s. But there were also new immigrants. During the 1990s, modest streams of Honduran migrants began arriving in the United States. This movement was very closely tied to the economic conditions of coffee production. When coffee prices dropped, Hondurans looked elsewhere for jobs; when coffee prices rose, out-migration decreased. Hurricane Mitch served as a further catalyst for the mass emigration of Hondurans to the United States in 1998. The hurricane killed 10,000 people and displaced over a million. In combination with a new coffee crisis that spanned from 2000 to 2003, a new wave of emigration took hold. By the 2000s and 2010s, a new threat incentivized out-migration: rising gang violence that left the Northern Triangle (El Salvador, Guatemala, and Honduras) with one of the highest murder rates in the world.

Within Latin America, certain countries also emerged as net migrant receivers. Costa Rica, whose economy has consistently been one of the most stable in the region, received more immigrants than it sent elsewhere between 1980 and 2020. This net positive immigration originated from its Central American neighbors, particularly Nicaraguans, relocating in search of opportunity and refuge. By the early 1990s, several other countries also became net receivers: Panama in 1992, and Chile in 1993. Brazil, Latin America's largest economy, became a net receiver in 2010.

On the opposite end of the spectrum were countries with negative net migration rates. Most of these countries were small: Haiti and the Dominican Republic in the Caribbean; the Northern Triangle countries and Nicaragua in Central America; and Bolivia in South America. El Salvador has consistently registered emigration rates eight to ten times higher than the regional average. Mexico, which sends out migrants and serves as a funnel for other nationalities hoping to move to the United States, was also an above-average net sender through 2022.[15]

The story of María Ruiz's family provides an individualized migration experience. While María was born in North Carolina, both of her parents were born in El Salvador. During the El Salvadoran Civil War of the 1980s and '90s, María's mother's family's lands were destroyed, and her grandfather killed due to mistaken identity. Her father, one of 13 siblings, became an orphan at the age of 12 and grew up in abject poverty. In the 1990s her parents left El Salvador for the United States, seeking better opportunities. Her father, who had the equivalent of a fifth-grade education, arrived first, followed by her mother, with the equivalent of a ninth-grade education. When María was three, the family returned to El Salvador, thinking they had earned enough to build a house. But employment was unstable and María's educational opportunities were lacking, so they returned to North Carolina.[16] In North Carolina her father is employed and at one point owned his own business. María recently became a college graduate. El Salvador lost out on their intelligence and ingenuity.

Understandably, the impact of immigration has been more substantial in some countries than in others. The share of remittances as a percentage of national GDP is one way to identify this impact. For Latin America as a region, the share of remittances increased between 1980 and 2020. In 1980, the remittance values averaged just 0.32 percent of GDP. By 2000, the share had risen to 0.92 percent, and then again to 2.5 percent in 2020. The total number may not seem significant, but the magnitude has tripled every two decades since 1980. The importance in El Salvador, Haiti, and Honduras has been particularly dramatic. By 2000, remittances already represented 15, 8.5, and 6.7 percent of their respective GDPs. By 2020, rates had reached 24, 21.4, and 23.6 percent, respectively. The money generated and sent back to these countries represented one-quarter of all the value of the goods and services produced within their borders.[17] Such a structure may result in material improvements for the people and communities receiving remittances, particularly in the absence of state infrastructure and investment, but remittance payment growth also increases dependence on remittances for everyday expenses like food, tuition, and medicine. It also fails to address the internal structural challenges related to inequality and development shortcomings, and security concerns that led to migration in the first place.

In 2020, NAFTA was superseded by a new agreement, the United States, Mexico, Canada Agreement (USMCA, or T-MEC in Mexico) and has been termed "NAFTA 2.0." The new treaty contains minor modifications in certain industries and more oversight over enacting labor laws. As a whole, however, the new treaty demonstrates a continued approach of more liberalized trade in the region that reduces tariffs and quotas, but discourages free labor movement across borders.

East Asian Financial Crisis, 1997 (Bangkok, Thailand)

In July 1997, Thailand devalued its currency relative to the US dollar. Contagion quickly set in, and a currency crisis emerged in Malaysia, followed by Indonesia and then South Korea. By 1998, the impact had permeated to several emerging economies beyond East Asia. The most significant was in Russia where the drop in oil prices and rising interest rates created a balance of payments problem. Russia owed more to its lenders now that interest rates were higher but brought in less revenue as oil prices were lower. Russia's 1998 economic crisis had a ripple effect in emerging markets around the world, including Latin America. In the end, the East Asian crisis marked a deceleration in Latin America's recovery, and in some cases, a reversal of gains made in the 1990s. Some economists even refer to it as the region's lost half-decade.[18] The shake-up also exposed Latin America's social vulnerabilities and ushered in a new political era to address persistent socio-economic problems of inequality and discrimination.

One of the reasons that the East Asian crisis was particularly newsworthy in Latin America was that the two regions had often been compared in their divergent approaches to development and growth in the post–World War II era. Comparisons really ramped up in the 1980s, as East Asia outperformed Latin America following the Volcker Shock. Both regions had received extensive funding during the 1960s and '70s, meaning that rising global interest rates in the 1980s negatively impacted both regions. But while Latin America plunged into the Lost Decade, East Asia's economies recovered more quickly. During Latin America's state-led period of growth that focused intensely on inward development, East Asia had opted for a more export-oriented model. This meant that in the 1980s East Asia had a more favorable trade balance than Latin America, helping the countries emerge more quickly from the global recession. Focusing on East Asia's relative success encouraged Latin America to enact a more market-oriented approach that would grow the region's export sector. This meant accepting the Baker and Brady Plans, expanding agricultural and mining export sectors, and adopting new currency and exchange rate strategies.

Reverberations to the East Asian crisis began shaking up the region in 1998. The timing of the restructuring meant that as East Asian countries endured their own currency crises, Latin American currencies and financial strategies faced a considerable external shock just as inflation was beginning to be controlled and consumer and investor confidence was returning. Early in its own journey toward stable currencies, and fresh off the spillover effects of the 1994 Tequila Crisis that left Mexico reeling, lower commodity prices and mistrust in emerging markets had the potential to tank efforts of stabilization.

After the 1998 Russian crisis, the Brazilian *real*, a new currency instituted in 1994, faltered. Investors, initially attracted to invest in Brazil because of high interest rates, became wary. The Brazilian government had used some of its foreign currency reserves to keep the real stable and utilized a **crawling peg** exchange rate, which *allowed the real's value to shift within a couple of percentage points of the dollar,* for as long as possible. But by 1998, Brazil's central bank could no longer jeopardize losing more of its foreign reserves, devaluing the real in early 1999. The currency quickly lost a third of its value. But, after the initial devaluation, the real stabilized, albeit at a lower exchange rate to the dollar.

The greatest upheaval was arguably for Argentina's economy, which was unable to stabilize as investment waned in the wake of the East Asian and Russian crises in the late 1990s. As global interest rates increased, capital inflows into Argentina slowed. In late December 2001, the nation defaulted on its debt. Just two weeks later, it devalued its peso by 30 percent and ended its fixed exchange rate policy (one US dollar for one Argentine peso). Trying to stem bank failures as foreigners and elites moved their savings out of Argentina, banks instituted withdrawal limits, *corralitos*, which restricted people's access to their savings and required them to withdraw funds in the devalued peso. If you were in Argentina in 2002, vendors strongly preferred to receive dollars, a more stable currency, as they were desperately trying to remain in business despite the dramatic economic downturn. During the first years of the twenty-first century, Argentine growth metrics turned negative, and unemployment surged above 20 percent.

In 2005, Argentina would restructure its debt, representing one of the most dramatic episodes in the country's financial history since the 1891 Baring Crisis. Now four years without receiving any bond payments for their investments, Argentina offered investors new terms. The country offered to exchange the old, unpaid bonds, roughly valued at US $65 billion, for new bonds, but at a rate 75 percent lower than the original bonds. The Brady Plan of 1989 had supported Latin American governments and lenders were willing to take a loss as loans were restructured, but investors balked at the Argentine offer. Nevertheless, most creditors ended up accepting the new terms: as a larger economy within the region, Argentina had the privilege to make demands that smaller countries did not.

Elsewhere in Latin America, the fallout from the East Asian shock in the late 1990s created hardships for the broader population. The market-driven approach may have increased growth and GDP in the early '90s, but wealth distribution continued to be unequitable. Extreme wealth concentration into the hands of political and commercial elites persisted and the Gini coefficient grew, meaning that the top income earners controlled an increasing share of the overall wealth. The growth also did not create jobs at the expected pace, with many reforms resulting in net job losses. The reality was that many Latin Americans continued to live in poverty. The global reaction to the East Asian crisis exacerbated these problems of income inequality and underemployment. In South America, the unemployment rate grew, and in Mexico and Central America, informality expanded. After 1998, when investment in Latin American capital markets declined, the gains from the early 1990s that had trickled down to the majority all but evaporated. Voting in democratic elections in the first part of the twenty-first century, Latin Americans made their discontent known via the ballot box. This environment created pressure on politicians to address some of the region's perduring challenges like income and land inequality, and educational shortcomings. Movements of marginalized Indigenous and Afro-descended groups added another set of demands on national governments: to explicitly address ethnic and racial discrimination and prejudice that further marginalized certain groups.

In Venezuela, politician Hugo Chávez centered his 1998 presidential campaign around the needs of Venezuela's poor. Running a populist campaign reminiscent of the 1930s, he vowed to counter the Washington Consensus. A case of "**Dutch disease**" challenged his ability to execute his promises. In Venezuela, oil deposits attracted foreign investment, driving up the value of Venezuela's currency and developing the oil sector extensively. Other sectors, as a result, were woefully underdeveloped and unable to compete with imports (due to the high exchange rate).

When President Chávez promised to direct oil revenues into social programs and nationalized electricity and telecommunications, high global oil prices between 1999 and 2008 theoretically created a sizeable opportunity for Venezuela. The results in addressing social problems were lackluster as many of the other sectors, suffering from years of underinvestment and neglect, were unable to meet demands. Venezuelan secondary school enrollments did increase, and the government directed a greater share of government resources toward social programs, but other development indicators worsened, even as they improved in the region as a whole. Up until 2005, the share of Venezuelans living in poverty increased, as did the share living in extreme poverty. Venezuelan infant mortality rates increased, and so too did the maternal mortality and neonatal mortality rates. Whereas Venezuelans enjoyed mortality indicators lower than the Latin American average in the 1990s, that ratio was higher than average by the 2010s.

Throughout the region, presidents campaigning with a similar *focus of addressing poverty and inequality were elected in the early 2000s. Eager to funnel commodity export revenues into public programming, the political transition* became known as the "**pink tide.**" Even though social programming agendas undergirded much of their campaign promises, these presidents did not follow Chávez's total about-face in Venezuela. Bolivia, for example, elected its first Indigenous president in Évo Morales. He vowed to help the urban poor, *coca* farmers, and Indigenous communities, but he also lobbied for full membership into Mercosur (whereas Venezuela was suspended from the trade bloc in 2016). Other prominent presidents considered part of the pink tide include Luiz Inácio Lula da Silva in Brazil, Ricardo Lagos and Michelle Bachelet in Chile, and Néstor Kirchner and Cristina Fernández de Kirchner in Argentina. Between 2005 and 2020, every country in continental Latin America except for Colombia had elected a leader who could arguably be considered part of the pink tide.

Until 2008, presidential terms coincided with an economic upswing in the region. It was not just oil, as most commodity prices were high, bringing in more revenue until prices dropped in 2014. In smaller countries, an additional income source, remittances, also bolstered economies. The result was more robust budgets that allowed government to enact more social programming. The average government spending on social programs rose to almost 19 percent of GDP in 2008. Because GDP also expanded, this meant real expenditures on education, medical services, and social programming increased substantially. The results, for the most part, were positive. Health indicators improved and poverty rates fell by 10 percent between 2002 and 2008, finally reaching pre-1980 levels in 2004.[19] In terms of education, Latin America faced an uphill climb to catch up to developed and East Asian countries. They started to make up some ground in the twenty-first century as matriculation and completion rates of pre-kindergarten, primary, and secondary schools rose. Until more significant educational strides occur, however, and conscious steps are taken to connect educational achievement to the formal labor market, it is unlikely that Latin America will see a significant reduction in income inequality. Despite all the social reforms instituted in the first decade of the twenty-first century, outside of sub-Saharan Africa, Latin American societies were and remain some of the most unequal societies in the world.

Notes

1 The Organisation for Economic Co-operation and Development (OECD) was established in 1961 to promote global trade and economic progress. Formed during the Cold War, OECD countries must be committed to both democracy and a market economy.
2 In the last five years of the 1970s, the share of national budgets directed toward debt payments ranged between –1 to 2 percent, Bulmer-Thomas, *Economic History of Latin America*, p. 398.
3 De Soto, *Other Path*, p. 143. De Soto's original book is entitled *El Otro Sendero*.
4 The World War II *Bracero* program brought in Mexican migrant workers to fill agricultural and railroad jobs, but persisted through 1964 and provided a strong social network for arriving immigrants.
5 Undocumented populations must be estimated through the 1980s. Warren and Passel, "A Count of the Uncountable."
6 The 1986 Immigrant Reform and Control Act (IRCA), which granted amnesty, had border policing provisions that proved counterproductive in reducing unauthorized immigration.

7 A distinction between refugees and asylum seekers in the United States is important. Refugees receive their status before arriving, whereas asylum seekers arrive and ask for permission to stay. Within the geopolitical framework of the 1980s, Cubans and Nicaraguans were often granted refugee status, whereas many Haitian and El Salvadoran asylum seekers were denied.
8 There were two notable plans implemented: the Brady and Baker Plan. Privatizations came with the Baker Plan.
9 NAFTA expired in 2020, being replaced by USMCA (United States, Mexico, Canada Agreement).
10 Brazil, Chile, and Cuba had initially agreed to the GATT when it began in 1948, with the Dominican Republic, Haiti, Nicaragua, Peru, and Uruguay joining in the 1950s. Argentina joined in the 1960s, but all other countries in the region joined after 1985.
11 Wars and conflict in the 1970s and '80s left the Central American Common Market ineffective. The Andean Community survived. Founding Andean Community members included Bolivia, Chile, Colombia, Peru, Ecuador, and Venezuela. Venezuela left the Andean Community in 2006, joining Mercosur. However, Venezuela was suspended from Mercosur in 2016. Chile became an observer between 1976 and 2006 and an associate member in 2006.
12 Belize was added in 1998 and the Dominican Republic in 2013.
13 Up to 70 percent of all corn produced in the United States was sold to Mexico by 2012. Osorio-Antonia, Bada-Carbajal, and Rivas-Tovar. "NAFTA and the Maize Belts."
14 Alba and Guzmán, *Making a Killing*.
15 ECLAC. "Population Estimates and Projections: Excel Tables," 2022 Revision, online edition https://www.cepal.org/en/subtopics/demographic-projections/latin-america-and-caribbean-population-estimates-and-projections/population-estimates-and-projections-excel-tables. Accessed January 22, 2024.
16 Interview with Maria Ruíz, April 10, 2015, "Nuevas Raíces," University of North Carolina – Chapel Hill. https://newroots.lib.unc.edu/items/show/159.
17 ECLAC, CEPALSTAT, indicator id 4016. https://unstats.un.org/sdgs/indicators/database/.
18 Ocampo, "Latin American Debt Crisis," p. 87.
19 Bértola and Ocampo, *Economic Development*, p. 250.

Suggested Media, Literature, and Digital Resources

"Latin American Migration Project (LAMP)." Princeton University. Accessed January 16, 2024. https://lamp.opr.princeton.edu/.

"Nuevas raíces: Voces de Carolina del Norte/New Roots: Voices from North Carolina." University of North Carolina. Accessed July 10, 2023. https://newroots.lib.unc.edu/.

Organization of American States. "Trade Agreements." Foreign Trade Information System of the Organization of American States. Accessed July 12, 2024. http://www.sice.oas.org/agreements_e.asp.

Salles, Walter, and Daniela Thomas, directors. *Terra Estrangeira* [Foreign Land]. New York: Fox Lorber Films, 2000.

Segura, Camila, and Daniel Alarcón, eds. "The Foreigner." *Radioambulante* podcast. October 2, 2018. Accessed January 1, 2024. https://radioambulante.org/en/audio-en/the-foreigner.

United States. International Trade Administration. "Research by Country." Accessed October 8, 2023. https://www.trade.gov/research-country.
World Bank. "World Development Indicator (WDI)." Accessed January 15, 2024. http://databank.worldbank.org/.
"World Inequality Database." Accessed January 15, 2024. https://wid.world/.

Selected Bibliography

Abud, Jairo. "La deuda externa mexicana y el Plan Brady: ¡Resultado y retórica!" *Investigación Económica* 57, no. 222 (1997): 17–45.
Alba, Alicia Gaspar de, and Georgina Guzmán. *Making a Killing: Femicide, Free Trade, and La Frontera.* Austin: University of Texas Press, 2010.
Banuri, Tariq, ed. *Economic Liberalization: No Panacea the Experiences of Latin America and Asia.* Oxford: Oxford University Press, 1991. Available through UNU-WIDER.
Bértola, Luis, and José Antonio Ocampo. *The Economic Development of Latin America since Independence.* Oxford: Oxford University Press, 2012.
Bruno, Michael. "Inflation Stabilization: The Experience of Israel, Argentina, Brazil, Bolivia, and Mexico." Cambridge: MIT Press, 1988.
Bulmer-Thomas, Victor. "Globalization and the New Economic Model in Latin America." In *The Cambridge Economic History of Latin America. Volume II. The Long Twentieth Century*, edited by Victor Bulmer-Thomas, John H. Coatsworth, and Roberto Cortés Conde, 135–66. New York: Cambridge University Press, 2006.
———. *The New Economic Model in Latin America and Its Impact on Income Distribution and Poverty.* London: ILAS and Macmillan, 1996.
Card, David. "The Impact of the Mariel Boatlift on the Miami Labor Market." *International Labor Review* 43, no. 2 (1990): 245–57.
D'Avella, Nicholas. *Concrete Dreams: Practice, Value, and Built Environments in Post-Crisis Buenos Aires.* Durham: Duke University Press, 2019.
De Soto, Hernando. *El Otro Sendero: La Revolución Informal.* Lima: Editorial El Barranco, 1986.
De Soto, Hernando. *The Other Path: The Economic Answer to Terrorism.* New York: Basic Books, 2002.
Devlin, Robert. *Debt and Crisis in Latin America: The Supply Side of the Story*, Volume 1027. Princeton: Princeton University Press, 2014.
Donato, Katharine M., Jorge Durand, and Douglas S. Massey. "Changing Conditions in the US Labor Market: Effects of the Immigration Reform and Control Act of 1986." *Population Research and Policy Review* 11 (1992): 93–115.
Edwards, Sebastian. *Crisis and Reform in Latin America: From Despair to Hope.* Oxford: Oxford University Press, 1995.
———. "Sovereign Default, Debt Restructuring, and Recovery Rates: Was the Argentinean 'Haircut' Excessive?" NBER Paper 20964, February 2015.
Fernández-Kelly, Patricia, and Douglas S. Massey. "Borders for Whom? The Role of NAFTA in Mexico-U.S. Migration." *The Annals of the American Academy of Political and Social Science* 610, no. 1 (2007): 98–118. https://doi.org/10.1177/0002716206297449.
Fischer, Brodwyn M., Bryan McCann, and Javier Auyero. *Cities from Scratch: Poverty and Informality in Urban Latin America.* Durham: Duke University Press, 2014.

Fishlow, Albert. "Some Reflections on Comparative Latin American Economic Performance and Policy." In *Economic Liberalization: No Panacea: The Experiences of Latin America and Asia*, edited by Tariq Banuri, 149–70. New York: Oxford University Press, 1991.

Hein, Jeremy. "International Migration and Historical Context." In *States and International Migrants*, 1st edition, 19–44. London: Routledge, 1993. https://doi.org/10.4324/9780429307539-2.

Joyce, Elizabeth, and Carlos Malamud. *Latin America and the Multinational Drug Trade*. New York. St. Martin's Press, 1998.

Kuczynski, P.P., and J. Williamson, eds. *After the Washington Consensus: Restarting Growth and Reform in Latin America*. Washington, DC: Institute for International Economics, 2003.

Levitsky, Steven, and Kenneth M. Roberts. *The Resurgence of the Latin American Left*. Baltimore: Johns Hopkins University Press, 2011.

Longmire, Sylvia. *Cartel: The Coming Invasion of Mexico's Drug Wars*. New York: Palgrave Macmillan, 2011.

Massey, Douglas S., Jorge Durand, and Nolan J. Malone. *Beyond Smoke and Mirrors: Mexican Immigration in an Era of Economic Integration*. New York: Russell Sage Foundation, 2002.

Musacchio, Aldo, and Sergio G. Lazzarini. *Reinventing State Capitalism: Leviathan in Business, Brazil and Beyond*. Cambridge: Harvard University Press, 2014.

Ocampo, José Antonio. "The Latin American Debt Crisis in Historical Perspective." In *Life after Debt: The Origins and Resolutions of Debt Crisis*, edited by J. Stiglitz and D. Heymann. London: Palgrave Macmillan UK, 2014.

Osorio-Antonia, Jos, Lila Bada-Carbajal, and Luis Rivas-Tovar. "NAFTA and the United States and Mexico Maize Belts 1994–2017." *Journal of Agribusiness in Developing and Emerging Economies* 10, no. 4 (2020): 385–402. https://doi.org/10.1108/JADEE-08-2019-0127.

Passel, Jeffrey S. "Changes in the Estimation Procedure in the Current Population Survey Beginning in January 1986." *Emp. & Earnings* 33 (1986): 7.

Rodriguez, Francisco. "An Empty Revolution: The Unfulfilled Promises of Hugo Chavez." *Foreign Affairs* 87, no. 2 (March/April 2008): 49–62.

Skoufias, Emmanuel, and Susan W. Parker. "Job Loss And Family Adjustments in Work and Schooling during the Mexican Peso Crisis." *Journal of Population Economics* 19, no. 1 (2006): 163–81.

Stallings, Barbara, and Wilson Peres. *Growth, Employment, and Equity: The Impact of the Economic Reforms in Latin America and the Caribbean*. Santiago: United Nations, Economic Commission for Latin America and the Caribbean, 2000.

Steiner, Roberto. "Colombia's Income from the Drug Trade." *World Development* 26, no. 6 (1998): 1013–31.

Székely, Miguel, and Andrés Montes. "Poverty And Inequality." In *The Cambridge Economic History of Latin America. Volume II. The Long Twentieth Century*, edited by Victor Bulmer-Thomas, John H. Coatsworth, and Roberto Cortés Conde, 585–645. New York: Cambridge University Press, 2006.

Thorp, Rosemary. *Progress, Poverty and Exclusion: An Economic History of Latin America in the Twentieth Century*. Baltimore: Johns Hopkins University Press, 1998.

Torre, Carlos de la. "Hugo Chávez and the Diffusion of Bolivarianism." *Democratization* 24, no. 7 (2017): 1271–88. doi:10.1080/13510347.2017.1307825.

Van Wijnbergen, Sweder, Mervyn King, and Richard Portes. "Mexico and the Brady Plan." *Economic Policy* 6, no. 12 (1991): 14–56.
Warren, Robert, and Jeffrey S. Passel. "A Count of the Uncountable: Estimates of Undocumented Aliens Counted in the 1980 United States Census." *Demography* (1987): 375–93.
Williamson, Jeffrey W. *Latin American Adjustment: How Much Has Happened?* Volume 4. Washington, DC: Institute for International Economics, 1990.

7 Recent History (2008–2022)

When does a particular event represent a short-lived shift and when does it mark a larger movement? Often only time reveals the answer to this question. That being said, Latin America's response and recovery to external shocks in the twenty-first century do seem to indicate an important regional shift toward more stability and steps in the right direction in terms of development gains. The two events highlighted in this chapter, the **2008 Global Financial Crisis** and the **2020 COVID-19 pandemic**, challenged regions across the globe, from Western Europe and Asia to Africa and the Americas. The region's response to those crises reveals an important deviation from periods before. Latin America did not plunge into a decade-long recession, and the economic downturns in most countries following these shocks were, for the most part, short-lived. The immediate impact of both events in Latin America shows the extent of the region's global connectiveness: it is even more integrated into a global economy than it was in the past. This chapter highlights noteworthy shifts and areas for concern in this most recent period of the region's history.

Latin American governments have long aimed to foster macroeconomic stability, striving for economic cycles that resemble undulating hills rather than jagged Richter scale lines created by an 8.0 magnitude earthquake. In the twenty-first century, there were two important developments. The region saw the emergence of government-funded programs that explicitly addressed persistent issues of poverty and inequality. It also saw a shift toward more developed financial structures that included autonomous central banks and spending, foreign reserves, and exchange rate policies that ran counter to the current economic trend. To make continued progress, countries will need to continue to turn toward countercyclical measures, reform tax policies, and address both high levels of informality and heavy reliance on remittances in the region. Finally, as much as history can provide a cautionary tale, countries should be mindful of increasing levels of indebtedness coming out of the most recent crises.

DOI: 10.4324/9781003283843-7

As a region, Latin America must also confront persistent social and economic inequities. Historically marginalized groups continue to register lower standards of living and face significant challenges to social mobility. Furthermore, while the gap between the richest and poorest 10 percent in each country has narrowed in some cases, the region continues to register high disparities both between rural and urban populations and between countries. Across the region, rural populations are three times more likely to live below the international poverty line than urban populations. This means that a family immersed in the informal economy and structures in a capital city like Mexico City, Santiago, or Lima will have more access to medical services and greater support for schooling than their compatriots living in remote, isolated communities, who lobby tirelessly for reliable water and electricity access. The differences between development indicators within the region are even starker. When using the international poverty line as an indicator, the rate of Haitians living below that standard in urban settings is 24 times higher than the rate of their Chilean counterparts. The difference is even more jarring when comparing rural populations: rural Haitians are 44 times more likely to be living in poverty than their Chilean counterparts. Ultimately each nation will need to evaluate what is right for it in the moment, but will also need to embrace a collective strategy to address regional concerns.

Global Financial Crisis, 2008 (New York City, United States)

On September 15, 2008, thousands of Mexicans gathered in central plazas at 10pm to usher in Mexican Independence Day celebrations.[1] In Costa Rica, El Salvador, Guatemala, Honduras, and Nicaragua, Independence Day celebrations were already in full swing. In South America, Chileans were gearing up for their independence celebration on September 18th. But the leading headline in Latin America (and the rest of the world) on September 15th in 2008 was not national pride, local parades, or historic reflections; it was the collapse of the global financial services firm Lehman Brothers Inc., the largest bankruptcy in the history of the United States.

In the United States, the early twenty-first century saw investment banks like Lehman Brothers turn to real estate as a solid investment. These large firms were backing smaller, mortgage-lending companies that worked directly with homebuyers. As demand for housing in the United States reached incredible heights, high-risk loans became more frequent as did predatory lending practices. By 2008, many new homebuyers found themselves in foreclosure. Unable to make their monthly mortgage payments, they lost their homes. As banks and investment companies tried to sell the foreclosed properties that they had repossessed, housing supply quickly outstripped demand, and for the first time in many years, housing prices fell. The mortgage bubble burst and investors quickly shifted investments to treasury bonds. The United States stock market lost one-third of its value and despite receiving millions of dollars in bailout support from the US government, Lehman Brothers was unable to weather the fallout. Like many other smaller banks and mortgage companies, when it declared bankruptcy on September 15th, it became another victim of the 2008 financial crisis.[2]

While Lehman Brothers was a US company, its failure had global ramifications that reached Latin America by 2009. Investors not only pulled money out of the United States mortgage market, but they also pulled investments and capital out of Latin America and other emerging markets around the world. Each of Latin America's eight largest countries saw subsequent reductions in GDP. As people became more wary of Latin America, currency rates and stock market prices fell in Mexico, Argentina, Chile, and Brazil. By this point in the book, this reaction should not come as a surprise. But, in a change of events, the 2008–2009 crisis did not create full-blown national financial crises in most of Latin America, nor did poverty and unemployment indicators increase substantially. The advances in the 2002–2008 period slowed and, in some cases, came to a halt, but in general, recovery was achieved by 2009 both in terms of standard production measures like GDP and development indicators like poverty rates and employment rates.

In past instances, such a global crisis often disproportionately impacted the region's most marginalized populations. By 2008, however, many Latin American countries had established a safety net system that reduced poverty and aided with development: **conditional cash transfer** (**CCT**) programs. At the end of the twentieth century, market-driven reforms helped stem inflation and brought some economic stability at the national level, but persistent poverty continued to encumber a substantial share of the region's population. In the latter half of the 1990s, Latin America's two largest countries, Brazil and Mexico, introduced CCT programs, *which deposited stipends into bank accounts of enrolled families so long as they met certain conditions considered important to reducing poverty*. By taking away precarity, CCT programs made gains toward reducing poverty in the region. Latin American poverty rates dropped from 44.1 percent in 2001 to a low point of 27.8 percent in 2014. The share of the population living in extreme poverty also dropped in the same timeframe from 12.2 to 7.88 percent. There was a slight increase in subsequent years, but rates largely stabilized up until the 2020 global pandemic. Equally notable was minimal variation in these trends across countries. Only Guatemala, Honduras, Mexico, and Venezuela deviated somewhat from this downward shift in poverty rates.[3]

Cash transfer programs have gained popularity globally in the twenty-first century, but Latin America was at the vanguard of their implementation.

The relatively strong business and economic cycle of the early twenty-first century to fund the programs as well as initial successes in Mexico and Brazil saw other countries launch CCT programs. By 2006, 18 different governments distributed cash to enrolled families (See Table 7.1). For poor families, these cash transfers were essential to daily life, representing about 20–25 percent of household income in 2010.

Specific conditions that enrollees needed to meet varied from program to program, but most centered on education, health, and/or nutrition requirements. Examples included children having to enroll and attend school or pregnant mothers visiting health clinics in order to receive cash payments. Many Latin American countries' CCT program goals connected to the United Nation's Millennium Development Goals set in 2000. The UN's goals were to eradicate extreme poverty and hunger; to achieve universal primary education; to promote gender equality and empower women; to reduce child mortality; to improve maternal health; to combat diseases such as HIV/AIDS and malaria; to ensure environmental sustainability; and to create a global partnership for development. The synergy between

Table 7.1 Initial conditional cash transfer programs in Latin America

First wave – founded prior to 2000
Brazil
Mexico
Honduras
Second wave – founded 2000–2004
Costa Rica*
Nicaragua
Colombia
Chile
Ecuador
Third wave – founded after 2004
Argentina
Dominican Republic
El Salvador
Panama
Peru
Bolivia
Costa Rica
Guatemala
Paraguay
Uruguay
Fourth wave – founded after 2010
Haiti

Source: ECLAC, "Non-contributory Social Protection Programmes Database: Latin America and the Caribbean." https://dds.cepal.org/bpsnc/cct. Accessed October 23, 2023.

Notes: * Costa Rica first program, implemented in 2000, only last two years. In 2006, they began a new CCT program.

Latin American CCT programs and UN goals meant that countries could often count on additional funding support from international lending institutions like the International Development Bank.

Key to the CCT programs' initial success was centering women and girls in the design and implementation. When governments provided cash to families, payments went to mothers. The logic, which in general was confirmed, was that mothers would be more likely to prioritize spending on goods and services that improved standards of living, such as higher-quality food and school supplies, than would fathers. Programs also directly addressed women in the conditions for cash transfers, requiring pre-natal visits to health clinics or awarding larger transfers for girls' school attendance than for boys'.[4] Programs tended to target women through informational and training sessions on nutrition and entrusted them with conveying their acquired knowledge to their social networks and the broader population. This knowledge and the requirements were at times at odds with communal practices or represented additional labor for these women to perform throughout the day, features that have led to critiques of the programs, but they substantially altered the lives of many enrollees.

The CCT programs are not without their weaknesses and critics, and their efficacy is limited by the quality of the services available to enrollees. However, they do seem to have kept poverty in the region at bay. Some conditions more directly address development indicators, while others contribute to a more holistic improvement. For CCT programs to continue to mature, the combination of conditions that need to be met must continue to be scrutinized. There is relative consensus that programs must also begin to focus on improving the quality of services, like school and health clinics, and re-evaluate the funding structure for such programs. When commodity prices were high, the programs were more easily funded. When those prices decreased, much of the funding to sustain these programs disproportionately impacted Latin America's relatively small middle class instead of its extremely wealthy – the top 1 percent earners who control 20 percent of the region's overall wealth. Revising the region's tax structure, particularly moving away from taxes that disproportionately burden the poor, such as sales or transportation taxes, toward those with a more equitable structure or even one that places a larger burden of payment on the rich, will be an important step toward ensuring a continued reduction in regional poverty and inequality.

The shift that several countries made in the wake of the Lost Decade and subsequent crises in the 1990s from **procyclical** toward **countercyclical** monetary (interest rates and money supply) and fiscal (spending and tax) **policies** helps explain some of the relative resiliency to the 2008 crisis.[5] For much of the latter half of the twentieth century, many Latin American countries followed **procyclical policies**, which *effectively followed the direction of current economic cycles*. During economic boom times, governments increased spending and lowered taxes, accepted and encouraged more capital inflows from lenders or investors, and increased the balance of payments. The problem with this approach, especially in a region like Latin America still heavily connected to and with a comparative advantage in many commodity markets, is that a procyclical response during economic downturns requires austerity budgets and fiscal and monetary shifts. In other words, the highs are high, but the lows are really low (see the 1982 Peso Crisis in Chapter 6). This volatility creates enormous social challenges and makes it difficult to sustain both growth and development on a personal and national level.

By 1998, at the same time that the first CCT programs were being implemented in Latin America, the ECLA began advocating for and several governments began introducing **countercyclical** monetary and fiscal policies. These *policies counteract current business cycles through choices that pull against the current trend.* One goal is to try to stem investor euphoria in times of boom to create more stability and trust during economic downturns. In Latin America, like in most developing economies, the most commonly used countercyclical tools address the amount of foreign currency coming into and out of the country. This variable is connected to exchange rates, interest rates, and the balance of payments. In controlling this monetary aspect, countries can reduce volatility at the national and local levels.

In terms of **exchange rates**, the *value of a currency relative to another currency*, there has been a more heterogeneous approach in Latin America in the twenty-first century. A few, mostly smaller, countries have fixed exchange rates, meaning that their value is pegged to, or moves in conjunction with, the US dollar. Some countries chose a target exchange rate but allowed a degree of fluctuation around that rate. This crawling peg means that the currency's value could shift within a couple of percentage points, but by design would avoid the volatility that can accompany a completely flexible exchange rate. This approach also preserves the fiscal and monetary autonomy of the national government that fixed and dollarized economies lack. In practice, however, these targeted exchange rates were difficult to achieve, and most countries shifted toward flexible exchange rates. Having a flexible exchange rate means that the official currency's value shifts depending on its global supply and demand. In these countries, the central bank plays a crucial role in implementing timely countercyclical monetary policies to mitigate volatility. With fixed or semi-fixed exchange rates, a central bank can lower its exchange rate to encourage exports or to attract foreign investment. With a flexible exchange rate, although a central bank can utilize interest rates and other tools to encourage money flows in one direction or another, it is the market itself that regulates the value of one currency relative to another.

Of the eight largest economies in Latin America, which represent 90 percent of the region's GDP, Chile led the way in implementing such countercyclical measures, but Mexico, Brazil, Colombia, and Peru also introduced countercyclical policies. In contrast, Argentina, Uruguay, and Venezuela maintained many procyclical policies. When the 2008 financial crisis hit, it became clear that one of the most effective countercyclical measures that countries had implemented was what could be described as a national emergency fund. Instead of spending all the foreign exchange coming in during the economic upswing of the first decade of the twenty-first century due to high commodity prices, investments, and the like, central banks built up the foreign exchange reserves. This set aside dollars for an inevitable rainy day. The 2008 crisis was just that sort of economic downturn. Governments turned toward the foreign reserves to both stabilize currencies and to help meet government commitments (like funding CCT programs). To further turn the tide and shift out of the crisis, some governments with countercyclical policies even created tax incentives. The result in 2008 for most countries was an economic downturn that was shorter and less dramatic than in crises past. Those countries with countercyclical policies fared even better.[6]

Governments encountered another challenge in 2014 when commodity prices fell. One country with procyclical policies that failed to truly recover was Venezuela. When oil prices declined, Venezuela's economy, an oil producer, suffered. The economy continued to contract, losing 45 percent of its value by 2018. Residents found themselves mired in high inflation, a shrinking economy, with poor access to healthcare, and facing political repression. Although the Chávez and Maduro governments' pink tide (see Chapter 6) campaigns catered to Venezuela's most vulnerable populations, the inability to control inflation, address shortages, generate jobs, and secure free elections created mass protests. The political, economic, and social stress was so high that millions of Venezuelans left the country: roughly 20 percent of Venezuela's population had emigrated or fled by 2018, many seeking refuge in the neighboring countries of Colombia and Brazil. On the eve of the next external shock, the 2020 global pandemic, Venezuelans already faced significant challenges. Other countries did not fare as poorly, but the heyday of CCT programs waned in the second decade of the twenty-first century.

COVID-19 Pandemic, 2020 (Global)

In December 2019, a new, highly contagious and deadly virus began ravaging China. By January and February of the following year, its global spread was apparent and in March 2020, the COVID-19 global pandemic was declared. It shut down borders and stopped all but the most essential work. Masking mitigated some risks, but government-mandated lockdowns emptied city streets, and shifted schooling and work, when possible, into remote settings. By August and September of 2020, the virus was reaching a peak in Latin America. When economies began to reopen somewhat in April of 2021 with the emergence of vaccine campaigns, the region recorded its crest of COVID-19 deaths. About 8 percent of the world's population lives in Latin America and the Caribbean, but over the course of the pandemic, Latin America represented almost 27 percent of pandemic-related deaths. Similar to the United States, the relative impact on Afro-descended communities in Latin America was greater, as was the impact on the poor.[7] Peru registered particularly high mortality rates, reaching 24.03 per million inhabitants in late April 2021, more than double the highest rate reached in the United States (9.9).[8] It is likely that Latin America's high urbanization rates elevated infections, but under-resourced health systems and the incredibly high inequality in the region also compounded the virus's deadliness.

The accompanying economic downturn was also swift and dramatic, with Latin American GDP decreasing by 7 percent. This was twice the global average and three times the drop in 1982 that set off the Lost Decade. The impact on informal and female workers was particularly acute. Women left the labor market more quickly than men and informal workers were limited in the work they could perform. However, despite the tragically high death rate and the relatively large loss in GDP, by 2022, development and growth indicators in most Latin American countries had returned to pre-pandemic levels. So too had formal and informal employment rates among both men and women.

Slow to make an economic recovery was Cuba. The island nation's economy was particularly challenged in the pandemic, recording one of the largest drops in Latin America and its greatest drop since the dissolution of the Soviet Union. As a country with a large tourism sector, lockdowns completely halted the hotel and dining sector in Cuba.[9] The country also faced a shortage of dollars and goods from the United States. Although the United States has a trade embargo on the island nation (see Chapter 5), money and supply remittances sent from Cubans living in the United States to family members in Cuba have served an important role in the Cuban economy and in the functioning of everyday life, particularly since 1996.[10] The slowing of the United States economy, thus, also reduced remittances to Cuba. While the Cuban scenario is unique due to the trade embargo, remittances have become an increasingly important component of GDP in many small countries throughout the region. The economies of El Salvador, Honduras, the Dominican Republic, and Haiti were particularly susceptible to the United States economic slowdown during the pandemic. As remittances continue to be an important component of GDP, these countries remain vulnerable to US economic cycles.

By July of 2021, social unrest reached its peak in the island nation and Cubans took to the streets to protest the government's response to the pandemic. "Patria y Libertad," which won the 2021 Latin Grammy song of the year, served as the protesters' anthem: "My *pueblo* asks for liberty, no more doctrines, / we no longer yell country or death but country and life / and to start to construct what we dream up / what you destroyed with your hands."[11] Cuba may have kept death rates low during the pandemic, but in July 2021, Cubans had minimal access to vaccines amidst a recent spike in COVID-19 death rates, continued to suffer from extreme medicine and food shortages, and experienced extensive power outages. Global shortages and the US embargo compounded the situation, but so too did the government's decision to develop its own vaccine rather than import those that were already developed. The high-stress environment also fostered Cubans' long-standing frustrations with the government's continued adherence to a more Soviet-style central-planning approach, dismissing any consideration of moving toward the socialist models of China, Vietnam, and Laos.[12] The Cuban government developed an effective vaccine shortly after protests, but a continued out-migration of Cubans suggests that discontent remains high.[13]

The pandemic not only revealed significant unrest with Cuba's status quo, but it also demonstrated downfalls associated with the region's high rate of informality. A feature of urban economies from the onset of independence, informality has become even further entrenched not only in the economic, but also in the social, cultural, and political fabric of the region. From street vendors and transportation companies to corner stores in what are technically informal neighborhoods, informality is an integral part of Latin American economies and the Latin American experience. As urbanization increased in the twentieth century and urban residents had to adapt to large-scale economic fluctuations, informality became even further entangled with the formal economy. In 2008, 15 of Latin America's 27 countries had informality rates above 40 percent, and seven had rates above 50 percent.[14] Rates remained high during the period and, as Figure 7.1 shows, contributed substantially to national production figures.

In the region where fiscal and debt crises have been consistent since independence, citizens and residents cultivated an entrepreneurial way to weather economic downturns that did not depend on government spending or interest rates: informal employment. Whenever times got tough, people could look to the informal economy to help make additional income. High turnover and an abundance of short-term jobs in the formal labor market in the twenty-first century meant that informal employment could even be more stable and autonomous than a formal-sector job. If your car is stopped at a stoplight in any major city in Latin America, the chances are that somebody with a water bottle filled with glass cleaner will offer to

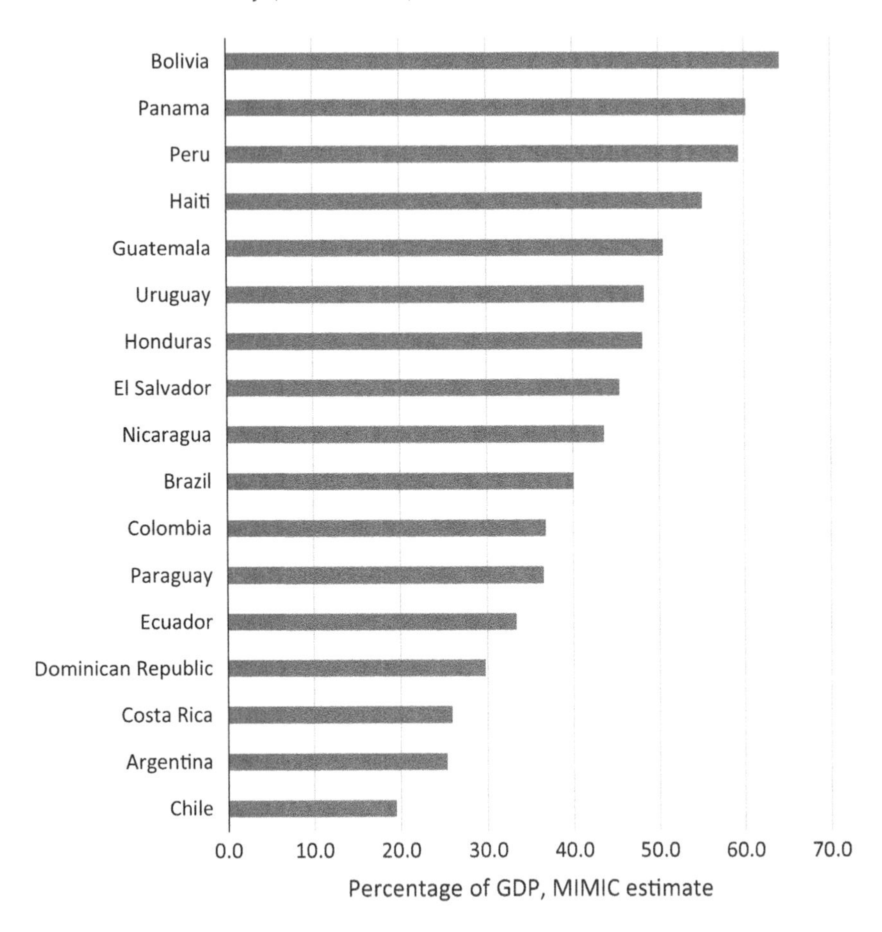

Figure 7.1 Latin America's informal economy: Estimated contribution to national production, 2020. Elgin, Ceyhun, M. Ayhan Kose, Franziska Ohnsorge, and Shu Yu. "Understanding Informality," Centre for Economic Policy Research, London Discussion Paper, 16497, Center, 20 August 2021. http://dx.doi.org/10.2139/ssrn.3914265.

clean your windshield before the light turns green. The structures that have emerged around recycling offer a more complex example. The practice of individuals specializing in activities from collecting recycling street-side on trash days to sifting through landfills to find recyclable material helps communities meet local, national, and international recycling and environmental goals and provides collectors with vital piece-rate incomes.

On the eve of the pandemic, informal employment was operating as a safety valve for roughly one in five Latin Americans. The problem during COVID-19 was that in-person interactions characterized much of this informal economy, so government quarantines and shutdowns severely hampered informal workers' job prospects. Being on the corner to wash a car window ceased to be a possibility. The pandemic's impact critically destabilized roughly 20 percent of the region's population.[15]

The initial shutdown exposed one vulnerability of having such a large informal sector, but the accompanying pandemic-related inflation exposed another. Inflation can act as a **regressive tax**. A *regressive tax creates a greater burden on the poor because everyone must pay the same rate, regardless of their income, meaning that the poor use a larger portion of their income to pay the increased rate.* Sales and gas taxes are some traditional examples of regressive taxes. Inflation, especially when it impacts food, transportation, and housing costs, creates the same burden. The 2020 pandemic introduced significant inflationary challenges. Reductions in global production created global shortages, as did disruptions in shipping and overland transportation. Even once a COVID-19 vaccine was developed and Latin American government vaccine campaigns started in March 2021, the region still faced substantial supply chain disruptions, something particularly challenging for the maquila industry (see Chapter 6). The escalation of the war between Ukraine and Russian in February 2022 further disrupted global supplies, prolonging the supply and demand mismatch.

Demand recovered more quickly than supply. In addition to lifting of lockdown orders, emergency cash transfers implemented by countries across the globe put money in the hands of consumers to jumpstart the global economy. This countercyclical measure served to counteract the abysmal drop in GDP and averted even further increases in poverty rates, but it also pushed up global prices on everything from workout equipment and refrigerators to food prices and fuel. In Latin America, the greatest increase was in food, fuel, and commodity prices, with a 30 percent increase in food prices in some countries![16] This was a particular burden to Latin America's informal workers, whose wages did not benefit from government-mandated minimum wage increases.

To be fair, there were moments even before the pandemic that exposed the region's challenge with inflation and informality. In 2013, two weeks prior to the inaugural soccer match of the Confederations Cup, a precursor to the World Cup, much of Brazil's transportation sector went on strike and widescale protests erupted in Brazil's largest cities. Some protesters asked, "what of my house, my life?" – a slogan connected to Brazil's CCT Bolsa Familia program, indicating dissatisfaction with the status quo and highlighting the continued need to create policies and programs to improve people's quality of life and standards of living. Brazil had spent billions in preparation for hosting the 2014 World Cup and 2016 Olympics megaevents, but it was the increase in bus fare prices that mobilized citizens.[17] Fare prices had been increasing at a faster rate than inflation since 2000, serving as a considerable regressive tax on Brazil's poorest residents. As the group most likely to use public transportation, the high fares placed a considerable burden on many households.

During the pandemic, Latin America's monetary response to increase interest rates to rein in pandemic-related inflation kept in line with the global response to try and rein in demand. Increasing interest rates, however, makes it more expensive to borrow money, and generally slows down the formal job market. The contraction pushes more people into the informal economy during an economic slowdown, meaning that both inflation and the monetary policies used to counteract inflation disproportionately impact informal workers. The conundrum is a no-win situation that highlights the need for the region to move away from such a large dependence on the informal economy.

In most cases, increasing interest rates did slow down inflation in Latin America, but what happens when increasing interest rates fails to work? That is exactly where Argentina found itself in June 2023, with interest and inflation rates *both* around 100 percent! What do you do when prices continue to double and the cost for a loan means incurring an impossible fee? As past crises have taught them, many Argentines have tried to convert their pesos into dollars. They hope to get ahead of a devaluation of the Argentine peso like the one they endured in 2001, but in making the switch, the peso becomes even more devalued. This process has brought about de facto **dollarization**, meaning that in Argentina the *United States dollar has become the preferred form of currency for everyday transactions*.[18] Some smaller countries in Latin America have undergone official dollarization, meaning that in Ecuador, El Salvador, and Panama, the dollar is the official currency.[19] In other countries with a heavy reliance on remittances, like Haiti, the Dominican Republic, Cuba, Honduras, and Nicaragua, or in areas where US tourists travel frequently, such as parts of Costa Rica and Mexico, semi-official dollarization has also occurred. In Argentina's case, however, dollarization was not part of monetary design and rather emerged from frequent economic crises.

Argentina is not the first country to undergo de facto dollarization in the twenty-first century. Bolivia had one of the highest rates of dollarization in the century's first decade, but there has been a return toward the boliviano, the official currency, since 2009. More recently, de facto dollarization has been Venezuela's reality. In 2019, when President Maduro faced an exodus of the population and a presidential and constitutional crisis, he opened the economy to allow for dollar transactions. Businesses began making the switch, and by 2023 most private sector jobs had switched to paying employees in dollars rather than bolivars.[20] While the pandemic disrupted the economy and 95 percent of Venezuelans were reported to live below the poverty line, emigration rates out of Venezuela began slowing.[21]

Trustworthy statistics on the state of Venezuela's economy remain difficult to come by, but the continued slowing of out-migration in the post-pandemic period suggests that important standards-of-living improvements have occurred.

Five years from now we will have a better understanding of the short- and medium-term impact that both dollarization and the pandemic had in the region. Fifteen years from now, we can start to evaluate the long-term impact of these events. Fifty years from now, we will be able to see the generational impact. How did remote schooling impact job opportunities and educational achievements for an entire cohort? What was the impact of women leaving the labor market for 18 months during the pandemic on their lifetime earnings and promotions? How did countries manage the increasing debt ratio incurred to avert national crises and counter the economic downturn? Did the region continue to move toward greater stability and combat poverty and excessive inequality? Only time will tell.

Notes

1 The official holiday for Mexican independence is September 16th, but the celebration begins at 10pm the night before, a time that symbolizes the original call to arms.
2 The federal reserve chairman during the crisis, Benjamin Bernanke, gave a four-part lecture series on the 2008 financial crisis at George Washington University in 2012. Those lectures are available via YouTube, https://youtu.be/E3fFg8XIS0k. Accessed October 14, 2023.
3 Guatemala experienced an increase in both rates between 2006 and 2014, Honduras between 2009 and 2012, and Mexico between 2006 and 2008. Venezuela's poverty rates are available for 2012, but there are no ECLA data available for subsequent years. Immigration rates based on data from Household Surveys Database (BADEHOG) suggest continued increase in poverty. ECLAC. CEPALSTAT. https://statistics.cepal.org/portal/cepalstat/.
4 Increased schooling for girls is one of the best indicators for increased development. Despite this, due to persistent gender wage inequality, many families opt to send boys to school because of the potential income they can earn over their lifetime as opposed to girls. Thus, targeting girls' attendance is a key feature of these programs.
5 This shift was facilitated by central banks becoming more independent.
6 Vegh, "The Road to Redemption."
7 Jarab, Cecchini, and Davis, "Decenio Internacional para los Afrodescendientes."
8 Mathieu, Edouard, et al., "Coronavirus (COVID-19) Deaths," Published online at OurWorldInData.org. Retrieved from: https://ourworldindata.org/covid-deaths.
9 Tourism is an important sector throughout Latin America, but represents a larger portion of GDP not only in the Caribbean, but also in countries like Mexico, Uruguay, Costa Rica, Peru, and Honduras.
10 The US Congressional Helms-Burton Act of 1996 penalized foreign national companies who traded with Cuba by preventing them from trading in the United States. This further restricted Cuba's global trade network.

11 Original reads "Mi pueblo pide libertad, no más doctrinas / Ya no gritemos patria o muerte sino patria y vida / Y empezar a construir lo que soñamos / Lo que destruyeron con sus manos." This particular line references the national anthem, which quotes the Cuban revolutionary and intellectual José Martí in his call for "patria o muerte."
12 López, "Cuba: The July 11, 2021, Protests."
13 "Cuba Net Migration Rate 1950–2024," Published online at https://www.macrotrends.net/countries/CUB/cuba/net-migration. Accessed February 14, 2024.
14 Bértola and Ocampo, *Economic Development*, p. 251.
15 The majority of Latin America's lowest quintile of earners are employed by the informal economy.
16 International Monetary Fund, "FAOSTAT: Consumer Price Indices." https://www.fao.org/faostat/en/#data/CP. Accessed January 24, 2023.
17 Many YouTube videos circulated during the protests. Some still remain accessible, for example, https://youtu.be/9orOOES7dMQ. Accessed July 31, 2023.
18 Dollars began to be used for some real estate transactions and savings in Argentina's urban environments in the late 1970s.
19 The Panamanian balboa and the United States dollar are both official currencies.
20 When Maduro was elected in 2018, the validity of his election was questioned. The president of Venezuela's National Assemby, Juan Guaidó, declared himself as Venezuela's acting president. There was much support behind Guiadó, but ultimately, Maduro remained president. The crisis, however, likely opened the door for changes in economic policies, such as dollarization.
21 Marco Arena, et al. "Venezuela's migrants bring economic opportunity to Latin America." *International Monetary Fund*. December 7, 2022. https://www.imf.org/en/News/Articles/2022/12/06/cf-venezuelas-migrants-bring-economic-opportunity-to-latin-america. Accessed January 14, 2024.

Suggested Digital, Media, and Literature Resources

Castillo, Paola, and Tiziana Panizza Montanari. *74m2*. San Francisco: LATINBEAT, 2018.

Economic Commission for Latin America and the Caribbean (ECLAC). "CEPALSTAT: Statistics and Publications." Accessed January 5, 2024. https://statistics.cepal.org/portal/cepalstat/dashboard.html?theme=1&lang=en.

International Monetary Fund. Food and Agriculture Organization of the United Nations. "FAOSTAT." Accessed January 24, 2024. https://www.fao.org/faostatt/en/#data.

Muniz, Vik, and Lucy Walker. *Waste Land*. Almega Projects and 2 Filmes, 2009.

United Nations. "We Can End Poverty: Millennium Development Goals and Beyond 2015." Accessed January 5, 2024. https://www.un.org/millenniumgoals/bkgd.shtml.

Select Bibliography

Adato, Michelle, and John Hoddinott. *Conditional Cash Transfers in Latin America*. International Food Policy Research Institute, 2010. https://ebrary.ifpri.org/utils/getfile/collection/p15738coll2/id/127902/filename/128113.pdf.

Alvarado, Sara Victoria, Pablo Ariel Vommaro, Jhoana A. Patiño, and Silvia H.S. Borelli. "Estudios de Juventudes: Una Revisión de Investigaciones en Argentina, Brasil y Colombia, 2011–2019." *Revista Latinoamericana de Ciencias Sociales,*

Niñez y Juventud 19, no. 2 (2021): 1–25. https://doi.org/10.11600/rlcsnj.19.2.4545.
Balen, Maria Elisa, and Martin Fotta, eds. *Money from the Government in Latin America: Conditional Cash Transfer Programs and Rural Lives*. London: Routledge, 2018.
Beccaria, L., F. Bertranou, and R. Maurizio. "COVID-19 in Latin America: The Effects of an Unprecedented Crisis on Employment and Income." *International Labour Review* 161 (2022): 83–105. https://doi.org/10.1111/ilr.12361.
Becker, Hilary. "The Impact of the COVID-19 Global Pandemic on the Cuban Tourism Industry and Recommendations for Cuba's Response." *Multidisciplinary Business Review* 14, no. 1 (2021): 71–83.
Bértola, Luis, and José Antonio Ocampo. *The Economic Development of Latin America since Independence*. Oxford: Oxford University Press, 2012.
Carbonnier, Gilles, Humberto Campodónico, and Sergio Tezanos Vázquez, eds. *Alternative Pathways to Sustainable Development: Lessons from Latin America*. Leiden: Brill, 2017.
D'Avella, Nicholas. *Concrete Dreams: Practice, Value, and Built Environments in Post-Crisis Buenos Aires*. Durham: Duke University Press, 2019.
Elgin, Ceyhun, M. Ayhan Kose, Franziska Ohnsorge, and Shu Yu. "Understanding Informality." Centre for Economic Policy Research, London Discussion Paper, 16497, Center, 20 August 2021. http://dx.doi.org/10.2139/ssrn.3914265.
Galindo, Arturo, and Victoria Nuguer. "Preparing the Macroeconomic Terrain for Renewed Growth." IADB Publications. 2023 Latin American and Caribbean Macroeconomic Report. https://publications.iadb.org/publications/english/viewer/2023-Latin-American-and-Caribbean-Macroeconomic-Report-Preparing-the-Macroeconomic-Terrain-for-Renewed-Growth.pdf.
Ha, Jongrim, M. Ayhan Kose, and Francziska Ohnsorge. "One-Stop Source: A Global Database of Inflation." *Journal of international Money and Finance* 137 (October): 102896.
Jarab, Jan, Simone Cecchini, and Harold Robinson Davis. "Decenio Internacional para los Afrodescendientes: Breve Examen en el Marco de la Pandemia de COVID-19 en América Latina y el Caribe." Santiago: United Nations, 2023. Accessed January 16, 2024. https://repositorio.cepal.org/bitstream/handle/11362/48660/S2300254_es.pdf?sequence=4&isAllowed=y.
López Segrera, Francisco. "Cuba: The July 11, 2021, Protests." *Latin American Perspectives* 48, no. 6 (2021): 37–43.
Ocampo, José Antonio. "Commodity-Led Development in Latin America." In *Alternative Pathways to Sustainable Development: Lessons from Latin America*, 51–76. Leiden: Brill Nijhoff, 2017.
———. "Macroeconomy for Development: Countercyclical Policies and Production Sector Transformation." *CEPAL Review* 104 (August 2011): 7–35. https://repositorio.cepal.org/server/api/core/bitstreams/347596b9-bf65-474f-8edd-bb1c1fef42ba/content.
Rennhack, Robert, and Masahiro Nozaki. "Financial Dollarization in Latin America." In *Financial Dollarization: The Policy Agenda*, 64–96. London: Palgrave Macmillan UK, 2006.
Stampini, Marco, and Leopoldo Tornarolli. *The Growth of Conditional Cash Transfers in Latin America and the Caribbean: Did They Go Too Far?* IZA Policy Paper No. 49, 2012. https://publications.iadb.org/en/growth-conditional-cash-transfers-latin-america-and-caribbean-did-they-go-too-far.
Vegh, Carlos A., and Guillermo Vuletin. "The Road to Redemption: Policy Response to Crises in Latin America." *IMF Economic Review* 62, no. 4 (2014):

526–68. https://www.nber.org/system/files/working_papers/w20675/w20675.pdf.

Vuletin, Guillermo, and Carlos A. Vegh. “To Be Countercyclical or Not? That Is the Question for Latin America.” Centre for Economic Policy Research, February 24, 2016. Accessed January 14, 2024. https://cepr.org/voxeu/columns/be-countercyclical-or-not-question-latin-america.

Yeyati, Eduardo Levy. “Financial Dollarization: Evaluating the Consequences.” *Economic Policy* 21, no. 45 (2006): 62–118.

Conclusion

Each Latin American country has its own unique economic history, but clear evidence of regional patterns, challenges, and structures have emerged over the past 220 years. Confronting how the region responded to global, national, and local events helps to understand these tendencies. The events elaborated in this text highlight the particular impact that commodity exports, national debt, volatility, marginalization, and informality have played in the region. However, these are far from the only regional tendencies, and future research will need to examine more closely the intersections between the region's economic history and environmental and (im) migration histories.

Commodity export economies and government approaches to expanding and including those sectors into national economic strategies were, are, and likely will remain, central to understanding the region. Latin America features vast natural resources, incredible biodiversity, and temperate and tropical agricultural zones. Industrialization, technological innovation, and economic transformation may substantially alter, but will not fully eradicate, those resources. In the new nations period, the allure of those resources brought in outside investors and saw the share of large-scale landholdings increase. During the export-led growth period, many national decisions revolved around connecting those resources to the global economy. In the state-led period that followed, the ECLA delineated how the commodity export sector featured in the development of global structural inequities. In the more recent past, the move toward greater economic diversification is one that includes new commodity exports like soy and oranges, alongside more traditional products like copper and coffee.

Expanding commodity export production required a considerable investment. So too did building new nations, keeping imperial advances at bay, and financing infant industry growth. In Latin America, those investments have often translated into high **external debt ratios**, *or the amount of money owed to outsiders as compared to GDP*. Countries have struggled to meet interest and debt payments and such a high debt burden has

DOI: 10.4324/9781003283843-8

often proved incredibly destabilizing. The debt responsibilities have frequently translated into reduced resources for residents, but defaults have reduced credibility in international markets. In effect, there is such a thing as too much national debt. From the 1825 Agreement between Haiti and France to Mexico's Cinco de Mayo and the 1980s, known as the region's Lost Decade, many of the episodes detailed in this book have some connection to the region's high debt.

National debt and commodity exports' susceptibility to global price fluctuations have contributed to Latin America's high volatility. Historic efforts to tackle global price fluctuations proved largely ineffectual and unsustainable through the region's Lost Decade. Recent history suggests that adopting countercyclical fiscal and monetary policies can lessen regional volatility. These initiatives have the potential to be politically unpopular, especially during economic upswings when the countercyclical measures can be seen as more restrictive in a region rife with inequality and many communities that have long confronted marginalization. The approach, however, might just lessen the duration and magnitude of economic downturns, providing the much-needed economic stability that has often eluded Latin America and its residents.

Terms like volatility, commodities, and diversification, not to mention exchange rates, dollarization, and capital markets, can seem disconnected from the ordinary person's daily life. These macro concepts, however, are intricately linked to everyday and individual decisions ranging from what food to buy for the family's nightly meal to deciding where and when to move. In calling attention to the challenges and opportunities that these somewhat impersonal events and trends made in everyday people's lives, this book also reveals the region's challenge with persistent marginalization and the growing informality, particularly in urban settings, that characterizes the region.

Individuals are uniquely affected by the broad and large economic changes in the region. Considering individual experiences collectively can yield important insights. It becomes apparent that traditionally marginalized groups often continue to be marginalized. Latin American colonial society was a highly stratified hierarchy and incredibly diverse both racially and ethnically. While some countries had larger Indigenous populations, and others concentrated Afro-descended populations, white, male, elites from Europe consistently occupied the top of the hierarchy. Independence offered little change in terms of the hierarchical structure, and by the end of the nineteenth century there was an even greater concentration of wealth among white elites. Health and education indicators, as well as land concentration indicators, show the minimal advancement of the lower classes relative to their elite counterparts. These inequalities continued to persist and at times even expanded in the twentieth and twenty-first centuries.

The logic that economic growth will trickle down and lead to economic development simply does not pan out when we look to Latin America. While each economic time period produced some very real economic winners, there were countless more individuals eking out an existence. After Brazil abolished slavery in 1888, the last country in the region to do so, recently freed slaves, as well as most Afro-descendants, faced substantial prejudice in getting jobs and had to confront housing discrimination. In the region's rural areas, agricultural laborers and peons endured exploitation and dislocation. Many marginalized groups moved to urban centers. Once the nation state expanded to offer social services more consistently in the twentieth century, like healthcare and social security, volatility often jeopardized those programs. An additional challenge for the region's poor has been the tax structure. The tax rates raised most frequently are those that most impact the poor's daily lives, while the progressive taxes, like income taxes, remain largely inconsequential.

Latin America's poor, however, are far from incapable. Their ingenuity is readily apparent in the complex informal economies that have developed in urban settings, particularly in the last 125 years. When veterans and migrants were unable to secure housing in urban centers in the late nineteenth century, they not only built their own houses, but created entire communities. If they found themselves on the edge of poverty or saving for something new, they sold lottery tickets, peddled wares brought from Europe or food cooked in cramped kitchens, or found other creative ways to bring in additional income.

As the twentieth century progressed and cities grew, Latin America became a predominantly urban region. Unsurprisingly, the role of informality in national economies ballooned. By 1980, one in five adults working in a Latin American city was employed in the informal economy. The ratio changed little in the following 40 years. The omnipresence of informality is unlikely to be eliminated in the region, because while 20 percent of the population is employed in the informal market, upwards of 80–90 percent of individuals buy or consume things generated in the informal economy.

When considered collectively, these trends point to a 200-year history of underdevelopment. Latin America has always been a little behind where it was expected to be. In the late nineteenth and early twentieth century, development was equated with modernization. State officials strove to increase the yards of cloth being produced or the number of new machines in operation. Latin America's actual output was less than its population and national income would suggest, meaning that even when new agricultural and industrial equipment was imported, it was not utilized efficiently. As the meaning of development transformed and came to encompass data like literacy and fertility rates, the region was still behind where it was expected to be globally. Latin Americans attended less school and had higher fertility rates than other countries with similar GDP per capita profiles. As we move further into the twenty-first century, our definition of development will likely continue to evolve. Maybe under these definitions Latin America will be able to shake the yoke of underdevelopment.

Given the challenges associated with climate change, it is likely that greater attention will be paid to the intersections between environmental and economic history. This text makes mostly tangential references to important ecological and environmental changes that occurred in the twentieth century. Early on, railroad tracks expanded the agricultural frontier. Later, industrialization and state-led growth harnessed hydraulic power and expanded highways and agricultural production. Today, mining and agricultural incursions into tropical rainforests have captured international attention because of the irrevocable flora and fauna destruction and the impact on global weather patterns. So too have crude oil explorations offshore and through remote areas. Each of these changes disrupted complex ecosystems and resulted in *unintended results*, or **externalities**. To understand whether the net economic result was positive or negative requires much more substantial and deliberate research.

If we are to understand how environmental history impacts day-to-day lives and decisions, we must look at the economic outcomes. Scholars have begun exploring the economic relationship associated with climate change by examining the intersection of natural disasters and (im)migration. This text, for example, highlights the number of individuals seeking temporary protected status after Hurricane Mitch decimated much of Central America. Less dramatic episodes can be just as influential. More frequent mud slides and droughts, for example, are also effective at incentivizing migration.

Natural disasters are just one of many factors to impact immigration and migration. Potential migrants also weigh considerations like political instability, social connections, family, wanderlust, and future economic prospects not only over a single lifetime, but also for future generations. This text has touched on these motivations in discussing European immigrants arriving in the Southern Cone in the 1890s and Mexican immigrants moving to the United States in the 1990s. The region's history with migration is much more complex. It includes foreign laborers brought in to harvest bananas and sugar cane. It includes marginalized urban residents accused of "vagrancy" who were forced to work in the agricultural sector. It also includes rural migrants moving to urban centers and working in formal and informal jobs to send money back home. Effectively, the region's immigration and migration history has much to teach us about its economic history.

Latin America's economic history, similarly, has much to teach us about both the region's general past and its place in global economic history. An interdisciplinary approach, one that values, carefully considers, and brings economists, historians, and other disciplines into conversation with one another, can provide that history. Who knows what possibilities such conversations will open for the future?

Index

Entries in *italics* denote figures; entries in **bold** denote tables.

For Product Safety Concerns and Information please contact our EU representative GPSR@taylorandfrancis.com Taylor & Francis Verlag GmbH, Kaufingerstraße 24, 80331 München, Germany

Printed and bound by CPI Group (UK) Ltd, Croydon, CR0 4YY
01/05/2025
01858429-0001